A Handbook of Medical Astrology

Jane Ridder-Patrick was educated at Kilsyth Academy and Hutcheson's Girls Grammar School in Glasgow and at Edinburgh and Heriot-Watt universities. She is a pharmacist, herbalist, practitioner of natural medicine and professional astrologer, with a practice near Glasgow. Her main interest is in integrating the essentials of naturopathy, the orthodox medical sciences, transpersonal psychology and astrology for practical application. She was a freelance broadcasting scriptwriter in West Germany for several years and is founding editor of *Astrology and Medicine Newsletter*.

CONTEMPORARY ASTROLOGY
Series Editor: Howard Sasportas

JANE RIDDER-PATRICK

A HANDBOOK OF
MEDICAL ASTROLOGY

ARKANA

Dedicated to
Alleyne and Max with love

*Und besonders für Malte ohne
dessen Abwesenheit ich dieses
Buch nie hätte schreiben können.
Mit Dankbarkeit und Liebe.*

ARKANA

Published by the Penguin Group
27 Wrights Lane, London W8 5TZ, England
Viking Penguin Inc., 40 West 23rd Street, New York, New York 10010, USA
Penguin Books Australia Ltd, Ringwood, Victoria, Australia
Penguin Books Canada Ltd, 2801 John Street, Markham, Ontario, Canada L3R 1B4
Penguin Books (NZ) Ltd, 182–190 Wairau Road, Auckland 10, New Zealand

Penguin Books Ltd, Registered Offices: Harmondsworth, Middlesex, England

First published 1990
10 9 8 7 6 5 4 3 2 1

Filmset in Monophoto Garamond

Printed by Clay's Ltd, St Ives plc

CONTENTS

FOREWORD
by Charles Harvey

This is a very important book. It provides both a comprehensive survey of the current state of Western astro-medicine and lays down valuable guidelines about how astrology can be used effectively in the healing arts. With her professional background as a practising pharmacist, medical herbalist, reflexologist and astrologer, Jane Ridder-Patrick brings an unparalleled level of experience and clear-sighted understanding of the ways in which astrology can be used as a practical diagnostic and therapeutic tool. She shows that astrology is a world view through which we may more readily attain to that ideal harmony between the forces of heaven and earth within us. Drawing on her broad knowledge of the world's astro-medical practitioners and the literature of the field, Ridder-Patrick has produced a book that will prove an invaluable introduction to the area for layman and medical practitioner alike.

The great astrologer and philosopher John Addey declared, 'From being an outcast from the fraternity of sciences astrology seems destined to assume an almost central role in scientific thought.' For this transformation of astrology's position in Western thought to come about it will be necessary for science to arrive at an understanding of the real principles of astrology. But equally, and as important, this development will be dependent upon skilled practitioners showing how astrology's ancient and revolutionary principles can be usefully applied to their own fields of science and art.

Much pioneering work has already been done in the fruitful application of astrology to depth psychology by those such as Carter, Rudhyar, Greene, Arroyo and Tarnas. Now in this work Ridder-Patrick, with her deep understanding of medical and astrological principles, opens the way to a new era of astro-diagnosis and astro-medicine. As the author says, 'There is a sense of renaissance in the air, and a willingness to learn, to co-operate, and to exchange our often strikingly different views.' What she is too modest to state is that if this is so, and if we are indeed approaching a time when, as Hippocrates is alleged to have said, 'A doctor without a knowledge of astrology will not rightly be able to call himself physician', then it will be in no small measure due to her own work as a tireless practitioner and correspondent with the whole astro-medical community. I would encourage all of you who are inspired by this book, and who would like to further the development of medical astrology, to spread the word and to join her in this vitally important work for the true healing of mankind and the world.

PREFACE

In this book I have attempted to bring together some of the major approaches that are or have been used in Western medical astrology. This is in no sense an authoritative rulebook. It is more an anthology of methods, information and ideas, some of which need stringent testing before being accepted into the mainstream of astrological knowledge. It is offered as a possible framework, a base from which readers can start to explore the subject for themselves and make their own discoveries.

Where possible, I have tried to use original material and the work of astrologers who have been involved in serious research in the field. My own work has brought me into contact with many of the world's practising medical astrologers. There is a sense of renaissance in the air, and a willingness to learn, to co-operate, and to exchange our often strikingly different views. We live in exciting times. The various strands are drawing together to provide a solid, consistent and reliable body of information on medical astrology that conforms to the first principles of both medicine and astrology. However unlikely it seems at this juncture, perhaps we are nearing the time in which, as Hippocrates is reputed to have said, a doctor without a knowledge of astrology will not rightly be able to call himself a physician.

Note: Instead of using he or she solely or alternatively throughout the text, which becomes either sexist or tedious, I have often used the colloquial form of the third person singular pronoun – they, them, their. My apologies to purists who will no doubt be pained, but rules of grammar, like any other crystallized form (♄) of spirit (♅), must, I feel, follow what needs to be expressed and not vice versa. It is comforting to know that many of the great writers have broken the same rules, among them Shakespeare, Goldsmith, George Eliot, Doris Lessing . . . to name but a few.

Kilsyth
April 1989

ACKNOWLEDGEMENTS

I should like to express gratitude to all who have helped me write this book, especially the following: Beata Bishop for her loving guidance, constructive criticisms and much cherished friendship; Gabriel Blass for his outspoken and helpful criticisms, his sharing of wisdom and for just being there when I needed him; Charles Harvey for his endless support, encouragement and warmth; Ingrid Naiman, whose work on stress and the elements I admire greatly, for her generous assistance and sharing of material; Olivia Barclay – without her zeal for horary I would have missed a valuable and fascinating branch of medical astrology; and Douglas Sissons for his Jupiterian munificence.

I

BACKGROUND NOTES

In any discussion concerning medical matters, we first need to define what we mean by health. Certainly it is not a mere absence of disease. It has a positive quality of radiant well-being, which is both subjective and objective. Unfortunately, health of this nature is comparatively rare; much more widespread, especially in the West, is the state that the Germans call meso-health. This is an uneasy limbo between overt clinical illness on the one hand and real vitality on the other. It is characterized by staleness, and a lack of sparkle, stamina, energy and *joie de vivre*. The World Health Organization defines health as a state of physical, mental and social well-being. This definition, however, omits the spiritual aspect of life, that fundamental human need for a meaningful structure on which to base and evaluate experience. The importance of the spiritual dimension has been underlined by the Swiss psychologist, C. G. Jung, who said that, of all his patients over the age of forty, there was not one whose problem was not essentially religious in nature.

The word 'health' comes from the same root as the word 'whole'. What does it mean to be whole – to be fully alive in every part of our being? The Chinese have a lovely image of man moving between the forces of heaven and earth with the goal of remaining in harmony with both. That is one of the best models for health that I have come across. For me, health is an awareness, an affirmation and an active participation in one's own destiny, with all the responsibility, pain and joy that that entails. It is an expression of creative free will within the boundaries of natural and cosmic events, so that the individual participates in the fullest possible unfolding of self in the context of the given life circumstances. Health is not a static or passive state; it is a process of becoming. It means taking up the challenge of existence and meeting life honestly and openly within the constraints of the individual character and situation. Implicit in this attitude is the willingness of individuals to participate in their own destinies, so far as their state of consciousness allows, and a readiness, which balances both flexibility and steadfastness, to adapt to the demands of constantly changing circumstances.

Astrology is one of the most accessible and reliable methods of pinpointing and analysing those factors which permeate inner and outer circumstances at any given moment, the individual's relationship to them, and the adjustments that need to be made to maintain equilibrium. From the state of inner harmony that comes from co-operating with these forces emanates health.

This view of health also includes the experience of disease and death, which are not necessarily enemies to be attacked and eliminated at all costs. Illness can be a teacher, as well as a source of strength and growth. Larry Dossey, in *Beyond Illness*, gives a moving account of an elderly patient, John, who was dying in an intensive care unit of pneumonia, blood poisoning and renal failure. Dossey writes:

As I stood there I was taken with a thought that made no sense at the time: *This man is healthy*. Lying helplessly, affixed to various gadgets, this gentle, wise, alert man seemed *beyond* the distinctions of health and illness. John seemed to transcend the easy classifications of 'sick or well', 'better or worse'. And he *knew* it too – he *experienced* this transcendence, radiating a kind of healthiness even when moribund.

An hour later John died – I am convinced, in good health.

MODELS OF HEALTH

The set of assumptions on which orthodox medicine is based has been called the biomedical model. This is composed of a mixture of two sets of ideas, those of Descartes, and the concept of reductionism. Descartes was a brilliant mathematician and philosopher who asserted that 'there is nothing included in the concept of the body that belongs to the mind; and nothing in that of the mind that belongs to the body'. The body is compared to a clockwork model. When the mechanism is functioning well, the person is healthy. Disease means that there is something wrong with the machine. This can be put right by tinkering with the appropriate cogwheels or, if that does not work, cutting off the offending piece, throwing it away and fitting a spare part.

Reductionism postulates that all phenomena, no matter how complex, ultimately arise from one primary cause. Taken to its logical conclusion, this means that for every disease, no matter who has it, there is one cause and therefore one correct way of dealing with it.

Since it is not possible in the world of the senses to do two things at once with any degree of efficiency, it is only by narrowing the focus of attention that progress can be made, whether it be in the arts, sciences or simply the concerns of everyday life. The wider the focus, the more difficult it is to investigate matters in depth. However, we also need a broad overview to prevent the development of tunnel vision, and to see how the subject under the microscope fits into the larger whole. Limiting research to the fundamental ideas of Cartesian philosophy and reductionism has produced a rich harvest of knowledge about the mechanical workings of the human body and many factors associated with disease. However, all models have a limited usefulness, for they are in reality artificial frameworks for examining the truth, and not the truth itself.

The biomedical model is now nudging the limits of its usefulness as the number of facts which it cannot explain away increases. It has led to the notion that patients participate very little in their states of health, and that disease is a visitation of bad luck from the outside in the form of, for example, 'germs' which cause a breakdown in the good working order of the body. There is a parallel notion that claims that unless tests show that there is a dysfunction or foreign body present, the patient is not ill. In other words, the limits of medical science are equated with the limits of the truth, which, to put it at its most charitable, shows lack of insight. Readers who have fallen foul of the system in this respect will no doubt have other designations. There is also an unspoken assumption and agreement between many patients and their doctors that the patient has the right to demand that the doctor make them well. In return, the patient hands over all the power and responsibility for their own body to the doctor. It is becoming increasingly clear, however, with the escalating costs and crises in health care, as well as an actual decline in real health, that this and other assumptions based on the biomedical model are no longer valid.

Many doctors and health workers, in the fields of both orthodox and alternative medicine, have realized this and are actively working on new concepts of health care which are not machine-oriented and which put the whole person at the centre of the treatment.

One of the foremost pioneers of the new approach is Lawrence LeShan, who has developed a model of holistic health based on the following principles:

1. A person exists on many levels, each of which is of equal importance.
2. The patient has systems of self-repair which are crucial to the prevention and treatment of that particular person's illness.
3. Individuals must be actively and knowledgeably involved in their own treatment.
4. Each person is unique and needs to be treated as such.

These ideas dovetail with the concepts of modern astrology. That the client is unique is self-evident from the natal chart; the ability to mirror back this uniqueness to the client is one of the major strengths of astrology, and is, in many cases, therapeutic in itself. Identification of the problem and then of the options available are the first steps in healing. The natal chart gives a detailed map of the inner territory, which is both a concrete starting point and an invaluable tool for the journey towards wholeness.

The natal chart may be looked at in many different ways. The most common approach nowadays is the psychological one, and a competent astrologer can make a substantial contribution in helping clients understand the make-up and dynamics of their own psyches. Some astrologers specialize in the spiritual approach, but it is unusual, indeed difficult, for a reading of any depth not to touch on this aspect. Spiritual does not refer to religious in the sense of organized worship, but rather goes back to its original meaning. The word religion comes from the Latin *re-*, meaning 'again' or 'back', and *ligere*, to 'bind' or 'connect'. Religious or spiritual here refers to self in the context of the whole, in other words the relationship between the individual's sense of meaning and purpose and that of the cosmos. A person without some sort of spiritual connection that makes sense to them is like a balloon without a tether. Astrology can show to any client, who is willing and able to look, their own particular connection with the universe and how it can be linked to their health.

However, one of the great dangers in recognizing the inter-relationship between patients and their own illness can be in presenting these insights to the person in such a way that it amounts to what can only be described as karmic terrorism. While it is true that a person has responsibility for all that happens in their life, whether it is disease or anything else, it does not imply blame. It is insensitive to say the least to add to a patient's burdens, which may already be considerable, by insinuating that it is all their own fault anyway.

The patient's involvement in the healing process is intrinsic to the practice of astrology. Each problem carries within it the seeds of its own resolution, and astrology can pinpoint and elucidate the problem or problems that need to be addressed. Each chart factor has the potential for positive and negative manifestations. It is only with the awareness and conscious co-operation of the client that a shift towards the more positive dynamic can come about.

ILLNESS – CAUSES AND TREATMENT

As LeShan said: 'A disease, from the viewpoint of holistic medicine, is a sign that something is wrong with your life. Your task is to find out what that something is and to take appropriate action.'

There are several reasons why a person may be out of harmony with the flow of creation. The most common is faulty maintenance at one or more levels. Another is that the individual is in the vulnerable and usually painful process of moving from one steady state of development to another. At the highest level, the esoteric teachings of many of the world's great religions speak of certain souls consciously taking on the burden of suffering and illness to lessen the load for others. It is, however, improbable that such a person will walk into our consulting rooms asking for advice, unless of course it is to do us a favour!

In treating a patient, before probing into the higher causes, it is usually best to work up the ladder of priorities and likelihood, from the body and emotions heavenwards. For example, the first thing to do when a person has been run over is to move the truck off the patient, not to call a priest. Similarly, where a patient is malnourished, the immediate task is to attend to the diet, leaving exploration of the relationship with the mother till an appropriate later date.

Certain signs – Virgo, Pisces and Scorpio – have been traditionally linked with the healing arts. I have used the characteristics associated with these signs to define the different therapeutic approaches.

Virgo

The most basic approach to health is the Virgo one, and it is the level at which I start with the majority of patients. It could be called 'following the manufacturer's instructions', and if we do not do that we are building our houses on sand.

The body, mind, emotions and spirit need certain conditions in which to flourish. If these are not met, ill-health and/or disturbed life conditions are the eventual results. Each level influences every other. An improvement or blockage at one level has a corresponding effect on the others, usually most marked in the level next to it in the hierarchy of: body-emotions-mind-soul-spirit. The correspondences seem to be rather like the Escher waterfalls that cycle endlessly in defiance of the laws of gravity.

Some people seem to get away with abusing the system for longer than others, but this is usually because they come from a good genetic background or have strong constitutions. At each level there must be correct input, throughput and output. This is most easily understood at the physical level. Just as it is inadvisable to run a Rolls Royce on one-star petrol, an unsuitable diet makes for less than optimal functioning of the bodily processes. This leads to disturbances in metabolism and excretion, which in turn leads to various degrees of auto-intoxication (self-poisoning). Where this is continued long enough and severely enough, organic disease is the outcome.

My practice lies in the disease badlands of Britain. To put it flippantly, the main problem with many of my patients is chips, chocolate and chauvinism. Change the first two – the third, whether as victim or perpetrator, may take a bit longer – and the results are often dramatic. There is no magic involved; all they have done is stop poisoning them-selves.

The inability to understand, process and assimilate experience, and then to let go and excrete the waste, lies at the root of many psychological and psychiatric disorders. Inappropriate or powerful input at the level of the psyche and higher can lead to health problems if not dealt with. It is just as possible to suffer from faulty metabolism and constipation at these levels as it is to do so in the body. While it is not always as easy to control mental and emotional input as it is to regulate food taken into the body, it is possible to modify it a great deal. Much of the material churned out by the media is the psychological equivalent of junk food. With care and thought a lot of it can be eliminated and more wholesome nourishment substituted. Indiscriminate and excessive ingestion of soap-opera sentiment, muzak and tabloid pap caters as little for sparkling psychological vigour as dining regularly at hamburger joints does for the body's needs. Used sparingly, as spices, a sprinkling of these experiences is fun, preserves our humanity and is a good prophylactic against po-faced health piety. But as a basic 'diet' they can hardly be said to provide the raw materials for creativity, original thought or authentic emotional response.

The natal chart shows up tendencies to dietary indiscretions as well as constitutional strength. It is often possible to detect patients most at risk from a poor diet. While almost everyone would benefit from a major overhaul in their basic diet, there are some people who respond particularly well to careful nutrition. Wherever Virgo is highlighted in the chart, especially where it is the sign of the Sun, Moon, Ascendant or sixth-house cusp, the naturopathic approach, which is in harmony with the basic nature of Virgo, is strongly indicated.

Naturopathy works gently with the forces and products of nature to co-operate with and support the body's own healing powers. Food is eaten as fresh, pure and unrefined as possible. Among the therapeutic tools are fire in the form of sunlight, pure air to fuel the lungs and bathe the skin, earth as the material constituent of food and as claypacks, and water for hydrotherapy.

The Virgo approach of naturopathy, I believe, is always appropriate no matter what other factors might be indicated in the natal chart, though the impact will be greater on some patients than on others. In the majority of cases it brings about significant improvements in health and well-being, probably because true understanding of the laws of nature is not widespread. It is hard to over-emphasize the fact, underlined by Dr Max Bircher-Benner, that the chances of success with all other therapeutic approaches are greatly enhanced where the liver is not over-burdened, the cells are well-nourished, and the bloodstream is a river of life and not a sewer.

However, in itself, the Virgo approach is not enough to bring about healing where the underlying problem is the need for transformation, or one of faulty alignment with one's innermost nature. There is a prevailing notion in current health literature that if we all lived in a pollution-free society, eating uncontaminated berries and leaves and taking adequate exercise, there would be no disease. Archaeological evidence, however, contradicts this. Arthritis, tumours and tuberculosis were present among the Ancient Egyptians, as well as in primitive man. Health is not simply a product of ideal physical factors, even if they are the foundation of the pyramid.

The negative aspect of the Virgo approach is to get locked into the cult of perfection and purity, and to end up unable to see the wood for the carrot juices and colonics.

Pisces

The next stage, or rather one that is fundamental to any therapy and ideally is present at all stages, is the Pisces mode. The greatest healer, as Paracelsus said, is love. Here sufferers are offered a haven of safety and comfort where they can bare their souls in the knowledge that there will be no judgements and only acceptance of them in the fullness of their being, as they really are, warts and all. The burden of pain, emotional and physical, can be lightened by sharing and merging with an understanding other. Listening, compassion, healing, and unconditional acceptance both by the healer and the Great Healer all belong to Pisces.

However, this mode has its dangers and limitations too. The first reaction of a caring person to the suffering of another is to want to take it away, and as such has great value in bringing out compassion in the carer. But that first response may not be the most appropriate if the treatment is only concerned with removing the pain, and does not address the root of the matter and the reasons for the breakdown in health. Where the sufferer is put into or chooses the victim role, and the carer becomes saviour, taking over the power and personal responsibility of the patient, it spells health for neither.

Scorpio

Scorpio is the sign most closely associated with doctors, especially surgeons – in its Mars rulership – and psychotherapists in its Pluto connection. This is the realm of the power struggle between life and death, leading to either physical or psychological transformation, or both.

At times illness can be seen to play a role in the process of individual unfoldment. There may be a development that can only take place through experiencing the conditions of some particular ailment. Often people who have been through the trials and sufferings of some life-threatening or debilitating disease express gratitude for the insights and maturity they have gained by having been forced to face that crisis. The Belgian Nobel Prize-winning physicist, Ilya Prigogine, has put forward the theory and mathematical proof of what he has called 'dissipative structures'. This theory may have great relevance in explaining these shifts towards new levels of health and awareness. The body functions optimally within the limits of certain closely regulated conditions of temperature, pH, chemical composition, etc. These conditions are kept in a state of dynamic equilibrium by the process of homoeostasis. This involves a network of feedback systems which, put simply, increases that which is too little and decreases that which is too much. Analogous processes are found in the structures of societies, civilizations and systems. In the evolutionary process, any entity, be it the body, psyche or society, is at certain points of time challenged by strong internal and external forces. As more and more stress is applied to the system, the central balance point which has up until that time formed the status quo, becomes untenable, as the system is unable to summon enough force to resist the changes and maintain the 'norm'. A homoeostatic shift becomes inevitable, and the resultant change leads to a higher order of organization. This is what seems to happen to some people, physically, mentally and spiritually, through the experience of illness.

The function of the practitioner working in the Scorpio mode is to midwife and accompany the client through this black, powerless, often terrifying and painful stage of destruction and – hopefully – rebuilding. Sometimes the practitioner becomes an instrument of destruction, where 'therapist' becomes '*the* rapist'. It is interesting to note in this connection that when the doctors went on strike in Bogota and in Israel that the death rate actually fell. It is almost as if a small proportion of doctors fulfil the role of state-registered executioners. In his book *The Combination of Stellar Influences*, Reinhold Ebertin tells of a certain family, the Hoffmanns, who through the centuries had been executioners, 'helping to transport convicted criminals from this life to the next'. When the demand for this service fell, the family produced mainly physicians and surgeons. Similarly, he cites the cases of families of butchers who, on becoming wealthier, started to turn out surgeons or engineers instead.

THE APPLICATION OF ASTROLOGY TO MEDICINE

Hippocrates (supposedly) wrote that a physician without a knowledge of astrology had better call himself a fool rather than a physician, and Culpeper (definitely) stated that physic without astrology is like a lamp without oil. Now these are pretty strong statements. What is it that astrology can offer to medicine that makes it so indispensable?

Astrology can be useful in providing insights concerning the diagnosis, prognosis and most effective treatment for individuals and their illnesses. It is in the ability to address the specific, individual case that astrology excels. The experimental data that provide the guidelines for orthodox medical assessment and treatment are based mainly on statistical averages. That gives us the average man who, of course, does not exist. Almost every assessment and treatment will therefore be only approximately right if that patient falls within the peak of the average, and potentially disastrously wrong if they happen to be one of the few per cent at the tail ends of the frequency curves.

Sir William Osler, a famous English doctor, once said that it was more important to know what sort of patient has the disease than to know what sort of disease the patient has. Practitioners of holistic medicine are starting to ask the question, 'Why is this particular illness happening to this particular person at this particular time?' These are issues which astrology is well-equipped to tackle. The natal chart can certainly demonstrate what sort of person has the disease, and transits and progressions show why, and why at this time. The natal chart will reveal, too, the likely reaction of the individual to stress. Since unresolved stress seems to have a major part to play in the aetiology of disease, this knowledge is of paramount importance. Chapter 2 examines this problem in some detail.

I do not think that we are advanced enough in medical astrology always to be able to make the connection between the patient as understood astrologically and the particular physical components of the disease. The thighbone-connected-to-the-kneebone approach of traditional rulerships, while it can give some interesting and important insights, simply does not hold water in most cases. Astrology is one of the finest and most advanced tools for understanding the individual psyche. This has come about through the work of skilled astrologers, such as Liz Greene, who also have a high degree of proficiency and scholarship in the theory and practice of psychology and psychotherapy. A great deal of work needs to be done by practising astrologers who are also medically fluent, whether it be in the Western, Ayurvedic, Tibetan or Chinese system, before medical astrology can reach the same degree of sophistication as psychological astrology. However, there are many link-ups with the body which have been pieced together over the years. Chapters 3 and 4 contain information which by tradition and/or experience has been shown to provide valuable clues.

The decumbiture chart is a specialized form of horary astrology which has been adapted for medical use. It is a useful tool to help evaluate what is going on at any one moment in the patient's life, and in particular the state of health. It is especially useful as it shows the practitioner's involvement in the treatment, a factor overlooked at one's peril, as well as the nature of the remedies to be given. Chapter 5 deals with this in detail.

A prognosis can be made by assessing the type of person who has the illness, and how they are likely to handle challenges and the need to adapt. Much information can also be gained from the timing of the transits and progressions, and from the decumbiture chart. In addition, the constitutional make-up will also determine which therapeutic measures are likely to be the most effective. The practitioner can then assess the factors at work and choose whether to oppose, assist or balance those processes. Chapters 6 and 7 on psychological therapies and materia medica provide further information on this subject.

REFERENCES

Bircher-Benner, Max, *Ordnungsgesetze des Lebens als Wegweiser zur echten Gesundheit*, Bircher-Benner Verlag, Bad Homburg and Zurich, 1984

Culpeper, Nicholas, *Culpeper's British Herbal*, reprinted Milner & Co., Manchester, ud.

Dossey, Larry, *Beyond Illness*, Shambala, Boston and London, 1984

Ebertin, Reinhold, *The Combination of Stellar Influences*, American Foundation of Astrologers, Monroe, 1972

LeShan, Lawrence, *Holistic Health*, Turnstone, Wellingborough, 1984

Further Reading

Capra, Fritjof, *The Turning Point*, Flamingo, London 1983

2

PREDISPOSITION
TO DISEASE

The inspiration for this chapter, and most of the astrological information in the section on individual response to stress, comes from the ideas and work of the American medical astrologer, Ingrid Naiman. As she publishes them privately, her books have not been readily available until recently. This is a great pity as they are packed with valuable insights, and are essential reading for any aspiring medical astrologer.

While it is becoming increasingly recognized in medical circles that certain conditions such as peptic ulcers, rheumatoid arthritis, cancer and heart disease have strong links with personality types and stress, it is Ingrid Naiman's basic belief that *all* illness is due to stress (although not all stress leads to illness). This stress is caused by an inadequate inner response to stimuli. When the individual deals appropriately with the need to adjust, arising from inner and outer pressures, there is no disease.

The following points need to be considered:

1. The structure and function of the body's defence system
2. The nature of stress
3. The individual response to stress

All these factors can be examined astrologically.

THE DEFENCE SYSTEM

According to Professor Robert Ornstein, a neurophysiologist at Stanford University, the function of the brain is not to produce rational thought but to defend the body. It constantly monitors changes in the external and internal environments, assesses whether or not they are threatening, and orders any adjustments required to maintain the stable internal state crucial for health and integrity. A growing body of experimental evidence shows that what makes an impact on the brain and motivates its instructions to the nervous system is not rational thought, but emotion. In astrological terms this brings us straightaway to the Moon. Emotions are triggered not by an objective response to an event, but by how the person interprets that event. That interpretation is highly subjective and not always 'accurate', that is, it might be perceived by others in a quite different light. The interpretation of changes in the environment depends on what kind of attitudes and belief system the person has built up, based on past experience.

It has been demonstrated that when we learn or experience something that is accompanied by an emotion, even if that emotion is totally unconnected with the experience, then every time that particular experience is repeated the same emotion will arise. First experiences seem to make the greatest impression, as do strong emotions.

We live in a sea of emotional currents, but are generally aware of them only when they are strong. This sea is described by the sign, aspects and position of the Moon in the natal chart. (And probably the sign on the cusp and planets in the tenth and/or fourth houses.) The influence of the Moon is greatest in childhood. It shows how a child is primed to pick up and generate emotions and is therefore a strong indicator of the emotional tone of the early years of life. During these early years we are constantly bombarded by new experiences which forcibly impress themselves upon us. How we receive these forceful impressions depends both on our own emotional atmosphere and on the nature of the experiences. The result is a deep-seated pattern of automatic response that forms the basis of behaviour for the rest of our lives. That is why, in medical astrology, the Moon is one of the most fundamental factors to consider.

A person with the Moon in easy aspect to the Sun, Venus or Jupiter is more likely than someone with the Moon in hard aspect to Mars, Saturn, Neptune or Pluto to generate a happy and optimistic learning atmosphere, and thus grow to be more trusting and open to outside stimuli. This has important implications for health, for many studies point to the link between negative emotions and decreased immunity, and therefore susceptibility to disease. Positive emotions are protective.

Figure 1 is a simplified diagram which sketches possible mechanisms for stress-related breakdown of health. I have added suggestions for the astrological rulerships.

Any changes in the environment are detected by the free nerve endings and special receptors, and messages are sent via the afferent nerves to the brain. These processes are ruled by Mercury.

The area of the brain responsible for processing this information and giving it meaning is the cerebral cortex, which is divided into two hemispheres. I believe that Jupiter may rule the left side of the cortex, while Neptune has obvious associations with the right. The left brain is concerned with linear, logical thinking, while the right brain deals with form, intuition, the relationship between things and seeing the whole picture.

The cortex has a rich network of connections with the limbic system, a part of the brain concerned with registering emotions and helping to maintain homoeostasis (a stable environment within the body); it is thus linked with the Moon.

It is in this cortico-limbic area that the process of emotionally based assessment of 'threat or non-threat', referred to above, takes place. The stronger the emotion connected with the incoming information, the more vigorous the response ordered by the brain. It has been found that negative emotions are picked up more quickly by the right hemisphere and positive ones by the left, which is what we would expect from the Neptune and Jupiter rulerships. Neptune is more selectively attuned to suffering and Jupiter to happiness and optimism.

Dr Margaret Millard, in a fascinating article on the brain and the immune system, seen from the astrological perspective, touched on the work of the Frenchman Renoux, who discovered that damage to the left side of the cerebral cortex depressed the immune system. Right-brain damage, on the other hand, caused increased activity in the white blood cells, which play a major role in the body's defence system. It would seem that the left side of the brain is concerned with the Jupiterian function of protection, while the right brain is more interested in connectedness and dropping the barriers between self and the other, a well-known Neptunian characteristic. The experiment seems to suggest,

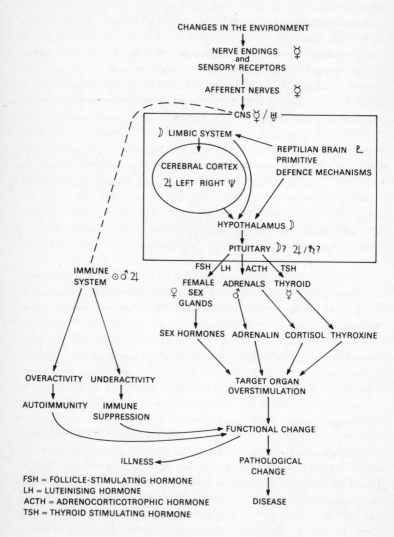

Figure 1 Stress-related breakdown of health

too, that there is some sort of dynamic balance between these two functions, so that in the healthy state neither the one nor the other is predominant.

Meditation and creative visualization, which are the province of the right brain, have been shown to stimulate the body's immune system and powers of recovery. It has been suggested that the reason these measures may work is that they keep the right brain so preoccupied that it does not have time to sap the vigour of the immune system. Astrologically this makes a great deal of sense. Neptune is notorious for its insidious undermining of health. However, if its creative potential is harnessed, re-aligned and expressed as in the use of such techniques as guided imagery and active imagination, the negative effects of Neptune, the victim, may be transformed into the positive aspects of Neptune, the saviour.

The pineal gland is a structure deep within the brain that, in esoteric literature, is said to be related to Neptune. Its function is unclear, but it has been shown to be light-sensitive. Experiments show that it is stimulated when a person watches the sun rise over the horizon. Light deprivation is linked with depression, negative emotions and lack of motivation, all of which give a predisposition to ill-health. A psychiatric experiment in the USA showed that exposure to high-intensity light can be dramatic in countering depression. Perhaps this is another way of working positively with Neptune.

The limbic system influences the hypothalamus and shares with it control of monthly and circadian rhythms of, for example, hormone levels, peaks and troughs of organ activity, digestive power and body temperature, as well as emotion. All these functions fit the symbolism of the Moon, which makes it the most likely ruler. The hypothalamus influences the immune system and also helps to regulate the activity of the pituitary gland. The pituitary gland is responsible for controlling the endocrine glandular function throughout the body. Esoteric tradition also places the pituitary in the Moon's domain. Dr William Davidson connects the anatomy of the posterior pituitary gland with Capricorn and the anterior pituitary with Cancer. Since the Moon rules Cancer, and the posterior and anterior pituitary glands are actually separate though interconnected entities, the two views need not be contradictory. Another view is that the anterior pituitary is ruled by

Jupiter and the posterior by Saturn. Certainly the fact that the anterior pituitary releases the growth hormone and five other hormones that are in various ways involved with increase and stimulation does indeed suggest a Jupiterian connection. The posterior pituitary releases an anti-diuretic hormone (ADH) and oxytocin, the former to do with conserving body water and the latter with contraction of uterine and breast-tissue muscles. Conservation and contraction are Saturnian characteristics. It may then be that the Moon passes on the baton of rulership to Jupiter and Saturn at the level of the pituitary.

The anterior pituitary gland regulates the female sex glands, which are closely linked with Venus. It also controls the thyroid gland which is associated with Mercury, and the adrenal glands which are ruled by Mars. Disturbances of hypothalamic and pituitary functions lead to suppression of the immune system and to hormone imbalances, which provide the perfect breeding ground for disease.

Recent research provides evidence of two-way links between the central nervous system and the spleen and thymus and other parts of the immune system. The most likely rulers of the immune system are the Sun, Jupiter and Mars. The Sun represents our vitality. Its natal sign, position and aspects show how we receive, contain and transmit the sustaining energy of life. Jupiter has already been considered in relation to the cerebral cortex, but it is also linked with the liver, the major detoxification (therefore protective) centre of the body. Mars has the important role of warrior defending the body's integrity. It is associated with the preparation of the body for action whenever danger threatens.

Pluto can be tentatively incorporated into this map as being linked with the so-called reptilian brain, the most primitive part of the brain, one of whose functions is to alert the body to the approach of danger. Pluto may also be linked with lower regions of the brain, mainly parts of the hypothalamus and mesencephalon, which govern behavioural patterns for the expression of defence and rage, as well as extreme docility. Defence, rage and the docility of the victim scapegoat are, of course, well-known Plutonian characteristics.

By using Figure 1 in conjunction with the birth chart, some valuable insights as to the inherent strength or otherwise of the individual's defence system may be gained.

FEATURES OF STRESS

Stress, or more correctly a stressor, is any stimulus that disturbs the status quo and calls on the individual to make some sort of response or adjustment. This can be achieved by an attempt to re-establish the balance via the homoeostatic mechanisms, if the stress applied is relatively minor in terms of impact or duration. Where the challenge is greater, the person needs to change and grow to accommodate and integrate the new factor. But in either case it must be dealt with in some way. The effectiveness of the individual's coping mechanisms determine whether the situation leads to growth or illness. As Nietzsche said, 'That which does not kill me, makes me stronger'.

Astrologically, a time of challenge and stress can be detected by observing the transits and progressions in the natal chart. One of astrology's aphorisms is that there are no events without significators, and no significators without events (either inner or outer).

This needs to be seen, too, within the context of the individual interacting with their environment, which also has its own astrological significators. For example, each of us comes from a certain family, lives in a town or district, which is in a country, on our own planet, Earth. Each of these – family, town, country and planet – has its own chart, which is constantly being activated by planetary movements and interacting with each individual within its sphere. It seems likely that epidemics and cycles of illness are just as much, if not more, bound up with these factors than with individual charts. While it is vital to keep these considerations in mind, it is often difficult, if not impossible, to examine the effects of these astrologically, as generally we do not have the required data.

A stressor can be anything from an employer's harassment to falling in love – though it is more often negative than positive. The person's subjective perception of whether an event is stressful or not determines the bodily response, not the objective reality of the situation. The subjective reality, as seen above, is dependent on in-built expectations and past experience.

The effects of stress are non-specific, the process being the same for everyone, regardless of the nature of the stressor, whether it be exposure to a toxic mother-in-law, junk foods, an unsatisfactory work situation or an accident. When something is registered by the brain as a threat (or excitement), the hormones adrenalin (USA: epinephrine) and nor-adrenalin (USA: norepinephrine) are released by the medulla of the adrenal glands. This increases the activity of the heart, slows down the movement of the gut, and shifts blood to the large muscles so that the person is ready to fight or run away. Astrologically this 'fight, fright or flight' response is ruled by Mars.

The body is geared for action, and the physiological effects of this response need to be used and discharged in some Mars-like way, either physically or emotionally, and preferably both. However, generally it is not socially acceptable to punch the boss or to run screaming from demanding children! Yet if some outlet is not found, the pattern of 'stress-reaction-blocked discharge' becomes a habit, and the result in the long term is damage to the body. It is not the 'stress response' activity which damages health; it is the lack of an appropriate expression for it. Properly discharged it is health-promoting. Anyone who has ever successfully run to the limits of their physical strength to protect their life and reputation will know that the resulting exhilaration is one of the greatest highs that life can offer.

Hans Selye, who spent most of his life working with stress, con-structed a physiological model of the reactive mechanisms which come into play whenever we are subjected to repeated demands. He called this the general adaptation syndrome (GAS).

Put in simple terms, the response to stress can be divided into three stages – alarm, resistance and exhaustion. The everyday example of food hypersensitivity may clarify this. When a person first takes food or drink to which they are sensitive (that is, the body sees it as a threat), the body will employ vigorous Martian measures to try to eliminate it or otherwise signal that it is unhappy about the situation. Some common reactions are skin rashes, vomiting, diarrhoea or headache. If that substance is repeatedly introduced into the body, the pituitary gland produces increased amounts of adrenocorticotrophic hormone (ACTH), which in turn causes the adrenals to produce more cortisol (see Figure 1). Cortisol damps down the alarm response and also gives a feeling of well-being. This is the second stage of resistance or adaptation, where it appears as if the ingested substance is not only not harmful, but is associated with pleasurable sensations because of the increase in cortisol levels. A situation of mild (and in some cases not so mild) addiction or dependency may arise. After a long exposure the body moves into the stage of maladaption and eventual exhaustion, when the mechanism breaks down. It is then that the person becomes clinically ill, although in actual fact it is only the culmination of a process which has been going on for a long time. The cycle of a transit can often be divided into three stages, which parallel Selye's G A S. In the first stage the problem is stated, often in the form of a crisis or some challenge which demands resolution. When the planet goes retrograde, there is a stage of resistance where the person tries to regain the status quo of the past. In the final, direct stage of the transit, resolution comes about one way or another. Depending on the nature of the planets involved, this can take the form of a divorce, a change of job, home or direction, or indeed illness.

Stress is also cumulative. In 1967 Holmes and Rahne drew up what they called the Social Readjustment Scale of life events, grading them according to their stressful impact. According to them, marriage (normally viewed as a joyful event, at least at the time), to which they assigned 50 points, is only slightly less difficult to cope with than suffering a major personal injury or illness, which scores 53, and is tougher than being fired at work, which rates 47. Research showed that people scoring more than 300 points within a year are 90 per cent more likely to become ill than those totalling less than 100 points. This gives a clear indication of the connection between severe stress and illness. Countless experiments on animals subjected to various kinds of stress have come up with the same results.

Astrologically, periods of stress are relatively easy to pick out in the natal chart. As the planets move on from their positions at birth to form aspects to the natal planets, they trigger, or correlate with, stimuli which need to be processed, assimilated and integrated into the psyche. It is a cardinal rule that influences impinging on the individual *must* be expressed somehow. Where this is done successfully, the person grows and unfolds according to their potential. Where it is not, tension builds up as the demands of the unused and unassimilated energy increase. Where the build-up of pressure goes beyond a certain level, which is specific for each individual at any one time, it overflows and is expressed outside the psyche as events appearing to happen out of the blue and/or as illness.

Selye said that people have a need to express their inherent nature without obstruction. This makes an interesting parallel to the first law underlying occult healing, given by Alice Bailey in her book *Esoteric Healing*, which states that all disease is the result of inhibited soul life.

A certain amount of stress is a necessary and enriching spur to greater effort, growth and achievement. The most stressful circumstance, according to Selye, is lack of motivation. Astrologically we come across a correlation to this in the occasional client who is ill, yet there is very little in the way of activity from transiting heavy planets to account for it. Often in such a case, most of the chart factors are found clustered within a few degrees of one of the quadruplicities or crosses. The person becomes ill precisely because there is nothing to provide a challenge. As Goethe said:

> Nichts ist schwerer zu ertragen
> Als eine Reihe von guten Tagen.

(Nothing is more difficult to bear than one good day after another.)

INDIVIDUAL RESPONSE TO STRESS

Studies in the USA and Israel, carried out by researchers like Pines and Kobasa, have shown that the attitudes which consistently determine good health are these: a strong commitment to self, work and family; the ability to see change as a challenge rather than a threat; a sense of control over the environment so that the person feels capable of dealing with whatever comes along; and an ability to make some sort of sense of what is happening and to feel that the challenge and effort are worthwhile.

On the other hand, people are more likely to become ill in response to stress if they feel alienated from the outside world, if they feel powerless, and if they lack a commitment to anything they do.

Ingrid Naiman has devised a system to assess the individual's susceptibility and reaction to stress and the inherent ability to adapt to challenge.

The key factors to examine are:

1. Planets in stressful aspect to each other, especially if the orb is tight

2. Planets in quadruplicities or crosses
3. The principal significators
4. Retrograde planets
5. Transits and progressions

The Aspects

The stressful aspects, in order of importance, are the square, opposition and quincunx, followed to a much lesser degree by the semi-square and sesquiquadrate. The tighter the orb, the greater the effect.

The Planets

When subjected to stress, the body makes physiological adjustments that prepare it for action. The energy that becomes available can be discharged as fight, flight or fright. How the individual is most likely to react may be assessed from various chart factors.

Ingrid Naiman divides the planets into three groups – the dynamic, the placid and the neutral. The dynamic planets, the Sun, Mars, Saturn and Pluto, are all yang energies. When challenged, they fight. The placid planets are the Moon, Venus and Neptune. They are yin energies and when challenged, they take flight. Depending on its position and aspects, Jupiter may be either dynamic or placid. The neutral planets are Mercury and Uranus. When they are badly aspected, they take fright.

The Dynamic Planets

The dynamic planets are the executors. A person who is under stress and who has hard aspects between dynamic planets will actively seek a solution in the outer world. This type of person is strongly committed to their sense of self and sees change as a challenge, to be met head on. Each planet has a different motivation, and this motivation will determine the type of action the individual is likely to take.

Where the Sun is involved in the situation, the person will look for the expert, someone who has achieved renown in their field. Only the best will do.

Mars looks for action, the quicker the better. It favours surgery, cauterization, acupuncture and any such vigorous, heroic and invasive measures.

Saturn is ambitious but cautious. It prefers a conventional, reliable and traditional approach, which has been well tried and tested over the course of time. It is prepared to wait for results. Chiropracters and osteopaths, as well as dermatologists, who are all ruled by Saturn, might be tried if they are appropriate to the patient's illness.

Pluto is goal-oriented and goes for radical and irreversible solutions, like amputation. It is painful to think of the number of patients I have seen with Pluto in hard aspect to the Moon (and sometimes the Sun) who have had hysterectomies or parts of the bowel removed. Where Pluto begins to manifest at a higher level, the person is usually willing to take on a long-term treatment involving detoxification and regeneration, like the Gerson therapy.

The Placid Planets

When the placid planets are in stressful aspect to each other, the tendency is to take flight to avoid confrontation. This does not mean that such people literally run away from the physical situation, but rather that, metaphorically, they stick their heads in the sand like ostriches and hope that the problem will somehow go away without their having to do anything about it. It sometimes does, and recently denial has come to be regarded as a perfectly valid coping mechanism, especially where the person cannot do anything to change the external situation.

In his book *Man's Search for Meaning*, the psychologist Victor Frankl wrote of his experiences in the Nazi concentration camps. He noticed that it was often not the dynamic, action-oriented types who survived. It was those who had rich inner lives that enabled them to accept the situation relatively calmly, and to find some deeper meaning for it. Where circumstances can be altered by willed action, it is an advantage to be able to act in a dynamic way. Where they are not, the inner reserves provided by the placid planets are more appropriate.

The Moon reacts according to deep-seated, habitual patterns acquired in the past. Taking the initiative is not its role, nor is any action which is outside the accustomed cycle of things.

Venus's prime motivation is to seek comfort, pleasure and self-indulgence. It is lazy and will try to avoid confrontation at all costs. If it does have to take action, it will do so by trying to neutralize the threat by seducing it and winning it over to its side.

Jupiter's more negative characteristics are complacency, over-optimism and extravagance. It often does not react because it is confident that everything will work out well, so why bother? When it does, in hard aspect to one of the docile planets, it is often with a misplaced largesse of feeling and sentiment which is ineffective in solving the problem.

Neptune, when it is acting negatively, is associated with dreaminess, fantasy and weak willpower. It just does not have the substance to deal with harsh reality and prefers to retreat into its own reality, which the world calls illusion.

People with a preponderance of hard aspects between the docile planets have a great barrier of inertia to overcome. They live in a subjective reality, and it is hard for them to be effective in the outer world. They can spend a great deal of time with plans and dreams of how to rescue themselves, but often lack the drive necessary to carry out these schemes.

The Neutral Planets

The neutral planets under stress may adapt, or, where hard aspects are involved, become tense and irritable. The person may even collapse from strain if the nervous system is over-stimulated.

Mercury is concerned with collecting information and passing it on. It tends to take on the coloration of whichever planet it most closely aspects, and thus the original message can get muddied with the bias of the other planet or planets concerned.

Uranus's function is to connect spirit to matter and to co-ordinate systems. Where it is badly aspected, there is a disruption of rhythm throughout the body.

Where Mercury and Uranus are in hard aspect there can be a defect in the flow between the intention and its realization. In practical terms this can result in the person running around flapping like a frightened hen (usually mentally, but it can take on a physical form too), unable to make a decision either to run away or to stay and fight it out.

Aspects between Mixed Groups

Where there are hard aspects between the dynamic and the placid planets, the active energy of the one is hampered by the inertia of the other. There is a pull between fight and flight. It is a bit like trying to run through thigh-deep mud. The square between Mars and Neptune has been called *the* pathological aspect, as Mars is the most active planet and Neptune the most passive and self-denying. Neptune dissipates the energy of Mars and undermines the body's ability and drive to defend itself. The Mars/Neptune midpoint is also an important health hazard, and any chart factor conjuncting or opposing it is significant. Transits to this midpoint need to be monitored carefully as they can be quite disruptive.

Where the neutral planets are involved, the person may also be unable to take action. They are closely connected with the nervous system, which can become overloaded and cause the person to 'freeze' into a state of paralysis, not knowing which way to go.

The Quadruplicities or Crosses

Emphasis on one particular quadruplicity or cross has far-reaching implications for health.

The Cardinal Signs

The cardinal signs are Aries, Libra, Cancer and Capricorn. This cross is action-oriented and projects its energy outwards, away from itself. The individual signs react to situations and stimuli according to their own particular natures, but all react vigorously. When a challenging situation arises:

> Aries attempts to make its mark on it.
> Cancer protects its own from it.
> Libra wants to relate to it.
> Capricorn tries to regulate it.

The cardinal signs are concerned with the defining of self through interaction with the environment. Medical problems may arise when they exceed their own boundaries and collide with other people and the environment. Typical examples are the contagious diseases and accidents caused by failing to recognize or ignoring the limits, whether they be physical, legal or emotional. The cardinal signs are similar in many ways to the dynamic planets. People with either of these emphasized need to learn to take responsibility for their actions and to recognize the problems they cause themselves and others (who often hit back) when they react with such energy. These difficulties can be approached by imposing self-discipline and purifying the motives which prompt the actions, so that the actions themselves become appropriate and ethical.

The Fixed Signs

The signs Taurus, Scorpio, Leo and Aquarius form the fixed cross, which has been referred to as having a centripetal action. This means that it has a tendency to draw in towards itself. What it has acquired it retains and is very reluctant to let go of. When challenged to change:

> Taurus holds on to what it possesses.
> Leo holds on to its glory.
> Scorpio holds on to its power.
> Aquarius holds on to idea(l)s.

The illnesses to which these signs are prone are cumulative in nature. Examples are congestion, growths, tumours, cysts, enlargements of a body part and blockage. Cancer is closely associated with fixity in the chart.

The problems of the fixed cross are very deep-rooted and difficult to shift, as they are bound up with a strong will, lack of response and often psychological isolation. The fixed cross, when it is operating at a high level, is a moving example of steadfastness, loyalty and service. Where this expression is not possible or is resisted, according to Ingrid Naiman, the person needs to move into the cardinal mode of action to let go of the emotional and physical toxins which have been stored up. Even though this can avoid the worst of the problems, this is very much a second-best approach. It does not go deep enough and is not a true expression of the person's inner nature.

There are some similarities between the placid planets and the fixed signs. The worst combination is several docile planets in a fixed cross, in very close orb, and retrograde, in the sixth or twelfth houses or in the second, fifth and seventh houses.

The Mutable Signs

Gemini, Sagittarius, Virgo and Pisces make up the mutable cross. These are the mental signs. The mind is constantly occupied and interested in new material, which each sign reacts to in its own individual way. When a stimulus appears:

> Gemini is curious about it for its own sake.
> Virgo wants to find a use for it.
> Sagittarius wants to evangelize and enthuse about it.
> Pisces accepts it, without surprise, as part of the universal whole.

The main problems which affect the mutables are due to excessive mental activity. There is a tendency to be out of touch with the reality of the situation in hand because the mind is busy scurrying about elsewhere. Mutable diseases are those of distraction – irrational fears, nervousness and irritability. The energies become scattered as the fear is that there is simply not enough time for all the things they want to respond to.

Most of the problems can be rectified by focusing the attention, doing one thing at a time and *finishing* it before going on to the next! These people need to filter the number of stimuli and concentrate on the wise use of what time and energy is available. It is useful for them to establish a rhythm in their daily lives. This helps to fix their energy and stops them spinning off at tangents. It also gives a guideline, often a lifeline, about priorities when they start to flap about distractedly, apparently having three hours worth of work to fit into one. One of the nightmares of strong mutable/neutral planet types would be to win a prize which gives them two minutes in a supermarket to grab whatever they want. Even that thought alone overloads the mental circuits of some to the point of paralysis. The following quotation from Alfieri might have been written for the mutable type. He wrote: 'Continuity of thought upon one single thing, and the suppression of every source of distraction, multiply in an extraordinary way the value of time.'

The neutral planets resemble the mutable signs and their problems can be dealt with in the same way. These people are generally easy to work with as patients, as they have insight into their own problems and respond quickly to treatment once their attention is focused.

The summary of the crosses in Table 1 is reproduced by kind permission of Ingrid Naiman.

Table 1. Highlights of the crosses

Fixed	Will	Right motivation and release		Emotional
Cardinal	Action	Right action and activity		Physical
Mutable	Thought	Right attention and thinking		Mental
Fixed	To feel	Magnetic	Unresponsive	Resistant
Cardinal	To do	Radiatory	Interacting	Energetic
Mutable	To think	Balanced	Restless	Flexible
Fixed	Moon	Venus, Jupiter, Neptune		
Cardinal	Sun	Mars, Saturn, Pluto		
Mutable	Mercury	Uranus		

Source: Ingrid Naiman, *The Astrology of Healing*, Volume 1, *Stress: The Cause of Disease*, p. 113.

The Key Significators

The most important significators are the Sun, the Moon and the Ascendant. The aspects they make, and the element and quadruplicity that each occupies, hold the key to the constitutional strength and potential for health. Ingrid Naiman reckons that the Moon accounts for 90 per cent of the factors which determine the constitutional type.

The Sun has an affinity with the cardinal signs. It relates to new situations and the need to deal with them. Afflictions to the Sun generally do not indicate deep-seated problems, but rather those for which some conscious solution must be found.

The Moon, on the other hand, relates to the past. It has much in common with the fixed signs. Its problems are more difficult to deal with than those of the Sun, as they are generally deep-seated, habitual and chronic. They often require depth psychology and/or spiritual counselling to shift them.

The Ascendant is more like the mutable signs. It is the individual's interface with the external and internal environments. Afflictions to the Ascendant can mean that the person needs to manifest, in some positive way, the nature of the planet or planets in stressful aspect to it.

Retrograde Planets

According to Ingrid Naiman, a retrograde planet is a point of tension in the chart. Where it is in hard aspect to other chart factors, the problem is likely to be deep-seated, and slower and harder to resolve than if it forms only flowing aspects. The person tends to cover the same ground over and over again, often repeating their mistakes. The time at which this pattern is broken is often when the retrograde planet goes direct by progression. This can be calculated by counting, in the ephemeris, the number of days from the birthdate before the planet goes direct. In secondary progressions, each day represents a year. For example, if Mercury goes direct ten days after the birthdate, the person will be affected by the change at the age of ten. Retrograde Mercury, Venus and Mars usually progress direct at some point during the life, but the heavier planets may not. The year in which the retrograde planet goes direct is normally an important but unsettling one. Esoterically, it has been suggested that retrograde planets point to unresolved situations and the misuse of powers and opportunities in previous lifetimes. The person has another chance in this life to rectify past mistakes. A bit of care is required, if this viewpoint is adopted, to avoid self-righteous moralizing over something which cannot be verified, as yet, one way or the other. The issues concerned can be seen from which planets are retrograde and which other planets make aspects – especially stressful aspects – to them. A summary of these are:

> Mercury – learning and the use of the mind
> Venus – relationships and love
> Mars – the use of initiative and energy
> Jupiter – the spiritual path
> Saturn – responsibility
> Uranus – revolt instead of revolution
> Neptune – ideals and psychic gifts
> Pluto – the use of power

The Sun and Moon, of course, cannot be retrograde.

REFERENCES

Bailey, Alice, *Esoteric Healing*, Lucis Press, London, 1984

Davidson, Dr William, *Medical Lectures*, Astrological Bureau, Monroe, 1973

Frankl, Victor, *Man's Search for Meaning*, Washington Square Press, New York, 1984

Holmes, T. H., and Rahne, R. H., 'The Social Readjustment Rating Scale' in *Journal for Psychosomatic Research*, No. 11, 1967, pp. 213–18

Kobasa, S. C., 'Stressful Life Events, Personality and Health: An Enquiry into Hardiness' in *Journal of Personality and Social Psychology*, No. 37, 1979

Millard, Dr Margaret, 'The Brain and the Immune System' in *Astrology and Medicine Newsletter*, No. 3, 1987, pp. 2–3

Naiman, Ingrid, *Stress – The Cause of Disease*, *The Astrology of Healing* Vol. 1, Seventh Ray Press, Santa Fe, 1986

Ornstein, Robert, and Sobel, David, *The Healing Brain*, Macmillan, London 1988

Pines, M., 'Psychological Hardiness: The Role of Challenge in Health' in *Psychology Today*, December 1980, pp. 34–44

Rosenthal, N. E., Sack, D. A., *et al.*, 'Seasonal Affective Disorder: A Description of the Syndrome and Preliminary Findings with Light Therapy' in *Archives of General Psychiatry*, No. 41, 1984, pp. 72–80

Selye, Hans, *The Stress of Life*, McGraw-Hill, New York, 1956

Further Reading

Hoffman, David, *The Holistic Herbal Way to Successful Stress Control*, Thorsons, Wellingborough, 1986

Simonton, Carl, Matthews-Simonton, Stephanie, and Creighton, James, *Getting Well Again*, Bantam Books, New York, 1980

3

GUIDE TO
CHART ANALYSIS

Let it be stated here once and for all that we are not dealing with symbols but activities, are not instituting metaphorical allusions but commenting upon urgent forces, quite capable of practical demonstration.

Heinrich Daath, *Medical Astrology*

One of the most difficult problems in medical astrology is trying to decide what each factor represents. The dividing lines between sign, house and planet tend to get blurred; rulership of structure and function are claimed indiscriminately by all. This has its counterpart in natal astrology, where the same personality trait can be described in several different ways. The themes of, say, Saturn conjuncting the Sun, Saturn in the fifth house and Saturn in Leo are similar and can lead to similar concrete manifestations.

However, Dr Harry Darling in *Essentials of Medical Astrology* makes a useful distinction. He says that the planets rule physiology, that is, the functions of the body, while the signs rule anatomy, which deals with body structure rather than how it works. Yet if we were to take it right back to commonly held astrological usage, then the planets would represent what is going on – the activities in the various systems of the body – in other words, the physiological processes. The signs would represent *how*, that is, the ways in which the planetary action is modified by a particular sign. Medically this is probably linked with the bio-chemical processes. For example, Mercury rules communication and therefore the nervous function. Where Mercury is in Aries, sensory input and nervous transmission would be expected to be quick and impulsive. With Mercury in Pisces, on the other hand, the nerve endings which pick up information from the environment might be over-sensitive to pain, touch, heat and cold, etc., and transmission of these sensations to the higher centres might not always be accurate. Extending the comparison with natal astrology, the houses would represent *where*, in this case the anatomical locations and structures. Dr William Davidson believes that signs are character, houses are fate. By this he means that the signs are what is inside a person – character, talent, disease tendencies – while the houses show environmental influences. This echoes what William Lilly, author of *Christian Astrology*, was saying at one point. However, both of them break their own rules on several occasions.

Dr Margaret Millard has found that planets in houses have a greater significance than anatomical rulerships. She quotes the cases of head injuries cited in Charles Carter's *The Astrology of Accidents*, where the first house featured in every instance, but none involved Aries, as might have been expected. In fact, in her research and in that of Douglas Bradley, Aries was involved to a much lesser degree than might have been expected on a statistical average.

The following are some of the common astrological correlations with anatomy, physiology and pathology. It is useful to bear in mind that there is a distinction between structure and function and that they belong to different astrological significators. However, because the demarcation lines are hazy and to save repetition, the houses and signs are taken together and the planets treated separately. There are many good astrological precedents for this.

It is more important to look at root causes and work out the likely effects from an understanding of physiology than to give endless lists of ailments. These are pretty meaningless anyway, as the same result can derive from a variety of underlying factors. A lesion or malfunction in one part of the body can show up as a symptom at a completely different site, and possibly in several seemingly unconnected areas. Conversely, if two people have the same symptom it does not necessarily mean that the causative factor is the same. Take, for example, jaundice, where the skin and mucous membranes take on a yellow coloration due to excess bilirubin circulating in the blood. It can have several different causes. There can be an excessive breakdown of circulating red blood cells. There can be obstruction of the bile duct by gall-stones, or inflammation or pressure from other adjacent organs as in, for example, cancer of the pancreas. It can be caused by liver damage from hepatitis, drugs or toxins. The end result is the same, but the underlying causes are different. Dr Davidson says that this is the beauty of medical astrology; it can pinpoint the true cause, which orthodox medicine, in most cases, cannot. It can also distinguish between pseudo forms of the disease and the real thing.

The following astrological correspondences with illness are, of course, not intended to be used for prediction. No responsible astrologer would ever scare clients with lists of possible future diseases. Furthermore, such predictions are likely to be inaccurate. There are many ways that planetary energies can be expressed and a breakdown in health is only one of them. The best preventative measures to ensure that health does not become a problem are attention to diet, hygiene, and the appropriate handling of the challenges of everyday life. Astrology is superbly equipped to give guidance in the last matter. Where I find these correlations of most practical use is in the insights they give in understanding the underlying issues when a person is actually ill or feels unwell. The symptoms point to the astrological factors involved and show what has to be dealt with to restore health.

THE PLANETS AND ANGLES

Sun

The Sun vitalizes
The Sun represents the vital force as well as the will to live. Its sign, aspects and house position indicate the vigour of the body. The Sun can be thought of as the light shining out of a light bulb. The type of bulb, however, will determine how bright that light is and how long it will burn. The light radiates most freely in the fire signs, then in the air signs. Water is more condensed and therefore a more difficult medium through which to manifest, so it takes a bit longer to 'charge up' again. Davidson says that people with the Sun in water signs, especially Cancer and Pisces, should not take frequent hot baths, as they tend to drain their vitality. The earth signs, which are linked with the densest matter of all, give tenacity rather than vitality, as they take in and give out

energy more slowly. Their light bulbs glow rather than radiate brilliance, but they do conserve what they have for longer and they can outlast the others.

Inharmonious aspects to the Sun can lead to fevers, eye disorders, loss of consciousness, haemorrhages, and heart, spine and back problems.

Anatomy and Physiology

> Vitality
> Immune system
> Heart function
> Spine and back
> Eyes, especially the right eye of a man and the left eye of a woman
> Individual cells
> Consciousness

Moon

The Moon responds
Davidson considers that, while the Sun indicates constitutional vigour, the Moon represents health, in that its sign and aspects show the flow of vital force rather than its quality. A disturbed flow will cause fluctuations in vitality and therefore ill-health. The Moon shows the instinctive, reflex actions and how the body adjusts to everyday challenges and stresses. (The connections between the Moon and health are covered more extensively in Chapter 2.) Moon patterns of reacting are set up in early childhood and tend to be fixed for life unless worked on consciously. Thereafter the Moon acts rather like the body's housekeeper, running on semi-automatic pilot. It is the single most important chart factor to consider when examining the health of the individual.

Lyall Watson, in *Supernature*, has reported on some interesting theories and experiments linking the phases of the moon with medical matters. According to one study, where the timing of more than half a million births was examined in New York between 1948 and 1957, there is a clear maximum just after a full moon and a minimum around the new moon.

An American doctor studying over a thousand cases of post-operative haemorrhaging found that 82 per cent of these crises occurred between the first and last quarters of the moon, with a clear peak around the full moon. Astrologically, the time around the full moon has always been regarded as unfavourable for surgical operations, as have times when the Moon is Void of Course (see page 113). Neither is it favourable to operate when the Moon is in the sign ruling the part of the body to be operated on, nor when it is in those signs opposing or squaring that sign. According to Dr Darling, the very worst time for surgery is in the three days preceding the new moon, as there are likely to be complications and the necessity for further intervention.

There are also suggestions that variations in blood pH and uric acid levels are lunar-dependent.

Moon problems can be water retention, discharges, vomiting and defective red blood cell formation.

Anatomy and Physiology

> Limbic system
> Pituitary gland
> Hypothalamus
> Lymphatic system
> Body fluids
> Mucous and serous surfaces
> Menstrual cycle
> Breasts and lacteals
> Fertility
> Stomach and alimentary tract, especially the assimilative functions
> Uterus in pregnancy
> Right eye of a woman, the left of a man

Mercury

Mercury communicates

Mercury is the messenger, the common linking factor between systems. It is therefore the natural ruler of the entire nervous system, which conveys information about prevailing conditions to the brain, processes it, and carries back instructions to other parts of the body.

The nervous system is made up of several parts: the receptors which detect changes in the internal and external environments, the sensory (afferent) nerves which convey information to the brain, the nervous pathways and functional areas of the brain itself, and the motor (efferent) nerves which transmit instructions to the muscles and glands. In itself Mercury is neutral, but it has the chameleon-like quality of taking on the coloration of any planet it closely aspects. Where Mercury is in aspect to the Sun, the ego becomes involved; to the Moon, family and habitual bias creeps in; to Jupiter, there is exaggeration; to Pluto, possibly a touch of paranoia; and so on. This means that Mercury's messages can sometimes be distorted, with the result that the brain processes inaccurate information and inappropriate commands may be transmitted. Response then does not match stimulus, and, especially if the heavier planets are involved, this can have important consequences for health, both physically and mentally.

Breathing, which involves a gaseous exchange, is also ruled by Mercury. Oxygen-rich air is drawn into the lungs and traded for air high in carbon dioxide. Mercury also rules gaseous exchange internally at the cellular level. Speech, hearing and touch, the means by which we communicate with each other, are related to this symbolism, as is the use of the hands. It is these faculties, together with the ability to reason, that gives man the superior dexterity and cunning which enables him to interact so skilfully with the environment.

Mercury illnesses are the nervous disorders, both physical and mental, communication problems and respiratory complaints.

Anatomy and Physiology

      Nervous system
      Mental faculties
      Breathing
      Hands
      Touch
      Organs of speech and hearing

Venus

Venus harmonizes

Venus is the principle of harmony, relationship and equilibrium. Translated into body terms that means homoeostasis and hormonal secretions. Homoeostasis (from the Greek *homos*, meaning 'the same', and *stasis*, 'standing still') is the body's ability to maintain the stable internal environment that it needs to function properly, whatever the external circumstances may be. One of the ways it does this is to keep the chemical composition of the body fluids constant through the action of the kidneys, which are ruled by Venus. The kidneys filter out all the unwanted soluble material in the blood and maintain the correct balance between acidity and alkalinity, and the amount of sodium, potassium and other ions in the body. Failure of the kidneys to function properly has serious consequences for health.

Inner conditions are also kept constant by the action of the hormones, which are secreted into the bloodstream by the glands. It is questionable whether Venus actually rules all the hormones as such. It is more likely that it rules the overall regulatory and secretory functions, rather than the individual hormones themselves. It does seem, however, to rule the female sex hormones. Venus has been traditionally linked with diabetes, so perhaps it is involved with insulin production and secretion, although some writers claim this function for Mars. I feel that the significance of Venus in maintaining health is greater than is normally credited.

Hard aspects to Venus can lead to stasis, lack of tone, congestion and swellings, cyst formation, diabetes and kidney disorders.

Anatomy and Physiology

> Homoeostasis
> Hormonal secretion
> Female sex hormones
> Ovaries and ova
> Kidneys
> Venous system

Mars

Mars energizes and defends

As in natal astrology, Mars represents the principle of energy and self-assertiveness. Heinrich Daath refers to it as focused heat. It is a centrifugal force which throws off, and a strong Mars, no matter how it is aspected, gives the ability to confront and burn out anything which threatens the integrity of the body. It is the natural adversary of Saturn, which slows down and cools, and of Neptune, which undermines the separateness of the unit, whether that is the cell or the individual. It governs inflammation, which is the body's response to injury. The injured area is first walled off with fibrin clots formed from the blood protein fibrinogen, which is ruled by Mars. Then white blood cells are attracted to the area in large numbers, and they ingest any foreign bodies and prevent infection while the damage is repaired. It is likely that Mars rules these white blood cells, as well as the haemoglobin which carries oxygen and carbon dioxide to and from the cells and lungs. Iron, the metal of Mars, is essential to the formation of haemoglobin. Mars also rules the adrenal function (see Chapter 2, under stress).

Body heat, which belongs to Mars symbolism, is produced mainly by the digestion of food and by muscular activity, both of which again are ruled by Mars.

The aspects of sexuality which involve aggression – arousal, increased blood flow, erection and penetration – as well as the organs involved, come under Mars.

Typical Mars disorders are fever, inflammations, sexual dysfunction, wounds, burns and skin eruptions, especially of the face. Mars has a strong connection with surgery and cauterization.

Anatomy and Physiology

Head area in general
Inflammatory response
Adrenal function
Body heat

Muscular tissue
Tendons
Sex organs and sexual function
Haemoglobin and blood fibrinogen
White blood cells

Jupiter

Jupiter enlarges and protects
Jupiter is protective, supportive and generous. Where it is poorly aspected it can be over-generous, leading to what used to be called a plethora – an over-fullness, usually of blood. Jupiter is strongly connected with the nourishing and protective properties of blood, and with the expansive, outgoing arterial system.

It rules the liver, which is the main organ for protective detoxification and for controlling fat utilization in the body. Jupiter rules fat metabolism. It is connected with the integrative processes of the left hemisphere of the cerebral cortex.

Jupiter afflictions can lead to blood disorders, liver problems, haemorrhage, stroke, fatty degeneration and hyperglycaemia.

Anatomy and Physiology

Liver function, especially detoxification and glycogen storage
Production of urea, uric acid and bile
Fat metabolism
Blood
Arterial system
Left brain
Growth hormone

Saturn

Saturn condenses, slows and cools
Saturn is the planet most closely connected with the solid matter of the body. It was formerly known as the 'greater malefic' because of its

seemingly life-threatening properties. While it is certainly true that Saturn is the planet furthest away from the fiery natures of the Sun and Mars, which carry the heat and impulse of life, without Saturn there would be no concrete form for this life energy. Saturn builds structures, in and through which the vital force can manifest. It is only where its energy is excessive or misplaced that problems arise. Saturn afflictions tend to produce chronic and deep-seated conditions, because the energy necessary to revitalize and move on is being obstructed.

It rules all the dense structural components of the body and the processes which produce them.

Typical Saturn problems are chronic skin complaints, stiffness of the joints and muscles, dental problems, deafness, depression, thickening and deformity, malnutrition, and the slowed functioning and atrophy of body processes and structures.

Anatomy and Physiology

Skin
Bones and joints
Teeth, especially the back teeth
Hearing
Induration
Ossification

Uranus

Uranus pulsates and co-ordinates
Uranus is the higher octave of Mercury and is also concerned with communication, this time between spirit and matter. Uranus represents how the individual is 'plugged into the mains'. Where the Sun can be seen as light radiating from a bulb, Uranus is what brings the power there in the first place. Without Uranus there is no life.

Everything that is alive pulsates. The pulsation of the heart is obvious, as is the rhythmic process of breathing. What is not so obvious is that every living cell pulsates because of its membrane potential. Smooth muscle tone is maintained by rhythmic pulsation. The whole digestive tract moves in co-ordinated pulsations to propel food particles from mouth to anus. Uranus rules all the rhythmic processes of the body.

These pulsations are regulated by the differences in electrical charge between the inside and outside of cells. The potential, as the difference is called, depends largely on the relative proportions of sodium and potassium ions. Potassium should predominate internally and sodium externally. The sodium group should be ionized with positive potentials and the potassium group with negative potentials. To quote Dr Max Gerson: 'In a sick body – mainly in cancer – potassium is inactive – sodium and minerals of the sodium group are ionized with negative potentials. On this basis all other abnormal processes develop as consequences.'

The most common keyword for Uranus in medical astrology is spasmodic, and that is certainly how it manifests pathologically when rhythms are disrupted. Uranus is concerned with the co-operation between individual units and systems, so that the whole can function in a co-ordinated fashion. Where one part operates at a different pace from the rest, the smooth running of the whole is affected. It is the same as when one process in the production line of a factory speeds up or slows down. The result is disruption. If one part is too slow, there is delay while the rest wait for the necessary components to arrive. If it is too fast, there is frantic activity to process the excess and prevent a build-up. In the body this leads either to paralysis or spasm, which is excess tone.

Some Uranus disorders are spasm, shock, cramp, ruptures, strictures, paroxysms and contortions.

Anatomy and Physiology

> Co-ordination of bodily activities
> Rhythmic pulsation

Neptune

Neptune unifies and dissolves

Neptune weakens and vitiates whatever it touches, as it is concerned with breaking down the barriers between the self and the environment in the wider sense. However noble that may be in terms of a spiritual philosophy, it is bad news for the body which relies on clear distinctions between self and not-self for its integrity and health. An afflicted Neptune can lead to auto-immune disorders.

Conditions which are difficult to diagnose, or are wrongly diagnosed, are often associated with a Neptune affliction. Nothing is as it seems when Neptune is around. It is connected with 'leakage' of vitality and with hypersensitivity. Dr Baldur Ebertin, in *Kosmobiologische Diagnostik*, suggests that it has to do with slackness or laxity of the aura. It is interesting that Davidson, in the late 1950s, mentioned the relationship between Neptune and fungi, viruses and other parasitic forms of life. Since Neptune has been in Capricorn (the polar opposite of Cancer which rules mucous membranes), there has been an upsurge in cases of gut candida infection (candida is a yeast), which has been linked with allergic and hypersensitivity disorders.

Neptune can also be linked with the pineal gland and right-brain function (see Chapter 2).

Some pathological manifestations of Neptune are coma, lethargy, drug and alcohol abuse, poisoning or the fear of poisoning, and general lack of tone throughout the body. There can be hallucinations and obscure diseases of psychic origin. Neptune is also linked with auto-immune disorders, and fungal and viral diseases.

Anatomy and Physiology

> Pineal gland
> Appendix
> Right-brain function

Pluto

Pluto destroys and regenerates

Pluto is concerned with survival at all costs. It has been described as a triple-strength Mars as it is also centrifugal in action, tending to great inflammation, forcefulness and destruction in the eliminative process. It has a concentrating action as well as an eruptive phase. The two processes that are closely connected with Pluto are childbirth and defecation. A foetus is a focal point of energized matter which ruthlessly extracts from the comparative stillness of the depths of the womb what it needs from the mother, whatever her state of health. When it has reached a state of ripeness where it can no longer be contained, it is expelled with great force into a new state of being.

A similar process of holding in a hidden place while concentrating, followed by expulsion, takes place with waste matter in the colon. Boil and abscess formation are related to the same symbolism. The distinctive feature of Pluto involvement is that the process is irreversible. The baby cannot return to the womb, any more than pus can be put back into the burst pustule. It is a one-way passage, with no turning back. If the expulsive phase fails for some reason, and the foetus, pus or faeces is retained, it can lead to toxicity and even death in extreme cases. It is futile to resist the cleansing effect of Pluto; it is ultimately life-giving, even though an old form has to be destroyed in order to create a foundation for the new. It is related to the cycle of nature – birth, growth, maturity, death and rebirth – and is said to be linked with Kundalini energy. Pluto aspects give a degree of violence and ruthlessness to the bodily processes regulated by whatever planet it touches.

Pluto transits bring to the surface that which was previously hidden and needs to be expelled, both physically and psychologically. Like other Pluto processes, this cannot be hurried and requires its own gestation period, which can be very wearisome and frustrating for the patient. All the patients whom I have seen with myalgic encephalomyelitis (ME), or post-viral syndrome, have had Pluto transits to personal planets or important chart features. Part of the bitter, but potentially freeing lesson of this devastating complaint seems to be acceptance, and coming to terms with what truly is, rather than what the socially adapted will desires.

Pathological manifestations of Pluto are abscesses, malignancies, fistulas and poisonous bites.

Anatomy and Physiology

> Reproduction
> Defecation
> Waste expulsion

Ascendant

Davidson compares the Ascendant to an electric wire and talks about its conductivity or resistance to the inflow of vital energy. In these terms, again like the Sun, the fire and air signs are the best conductors, with the water signs managing reasonably well, and earth proving the most resistant. This is why children with earth Ascendants, and most especially Capricorn, are often sickly early in life but become healthier later on.

The Ascendant is about interaction with the environment. It is the point of meeting between the internal world of the individual and all that is external. In natal astrology it has been compared to a lens through which the person views the world and through which the world looks back at them, or to the front door of the person's 'house'. Medically it is how patients perceive and receive their 'diet', in the ancient sense of the word. Diet used to mean anything and everything that was taken in and included not only food and drink, but air, thoughts, emotions and atmospheres. Seen in this way, it is easy to understand why fire, with its enthusiasm, and air, with its curiosity and readiness to relate, are good 'conductors'. They are generally open to interaction. Water tends more to self-protection, and earth to caution, which slow down the process of spontaneous exchange. These different ways of facing and coping with the environment have profound effects at the body level.

The Ascendant also relates to the moment of birth, and the sign on the first-house cusp, as well as planets aspecting it, can often throw light on the nature of the delivery and the atmosphere surrounding it. My first son has Scorpio rising and Uranus exactly on the Ascendant. Labour was protracted, as thunder and lightning stormed outside. There was high drama at the last moment, as the doctors decided that to continue without intervention would endanger the baby's life. He had to be extracted forcibly and abruptly with an electrical apparatus which applied suction to his head, then he was separated from me and rushed to an incubator to restore his birth colour of a deep navy-blue to a healthy pink. In contrast, my second son has the Sun conjuncting his Virgo Ascendant. Labour went like clockwork – I had a list of all the stages with me. It was a completely natural birth with no painkillers or medical assistance, and the sense of triumph, joy and light as he emerged was almost tangible. The entry into the world is of crucial importance, as it sets the precedent for all future dealings with the environment.

Midheaven

The Midheaven crowns the chart and represents our highest aspirations and ambitions in the outer world. Its sign shows the qualities on which we would like to found our reputation, our public image. Medically, Reinhold Ebertin suggests that the Midheaven is connected with the brain proper, by which he presumably means the cortex, which deals with consciousness of self. I have often found that an illness makes itself manifest – 'goes public', for all the world to see – when the Midheaven is transited by one of the heavy planets.

THE ASPECTS

In medical astrology there has been no attempt to discriminate between the various types of aspect. In general the hard aspects produce more health problems, although this is not invariably so. According to Dr Mario Jones, quoted in Robert Hand's *Horoscope Symbols*, hard aspects coincide with the onset of an acute illness which reaches a definite critical point, while the flowing aspects are linked with chronic illnesses which build up gradually, persist for a long time, but never come to a crisis.

Where one planet is said to afflict another, it means that it forms a difficult aspect to it. The outermost planet is usually regarded as the afflictor and the innermost one as the afflicted. Pluto can afflict all the other planets, while Uranus can afflict all except Pluto and Neptune as they are further from the Sun than Uranus. Mercury can only afflict the Moon and Sun. The most difficult aspects are the square, opposition and quincunx. The semi-square and sesquiquadrate are normally of minor importance, unless the chart has no or few other difficult aspects. The effect of the conjunction depends on the nature of the planets involved and other aspects to them.

Sun–Moon

The Sun refers to action taken consciously. It is a positive, creative force, concerned with actively facing and fashioning the here and now, which is always new. The Moon is a reactive energy, conditioned by patterns and experiences from the past. It responds rather than initiates. Where the Sun and Moon are in harmony, the creative energy and vitality are nourished by appropriate back-up responses and the basis for health is good. Where the aspect is a hard one, action and reaction are out of tune and the ground is prepared for unstable health. By itself, the hard aspect is unlikely to produce poor health. Davidson says that when the Sun and Moon are in opposition, the energy fluctuates, coming in waves. It is either high or low, and it is necessary to rest when it is absent and to push forward when it is available. Flowing aspects tend to give a feeling of being comfortable in one's own skin, while difficult aspects produce a deep-seated unease with the self. This can make life so uncomfortable that the person is driven to explore their own psyche in an attempt to find peace, which can be very positive and productive.

Sun–Moon aspects, either natally or by transit, can affect the eyes and the composition of body fluids – the blood, serum, extra and intra-cellular fluids.

William Lilly says that where the Moon is either in conjunction or opposition to the Sun, there is likely to be a blemish near one of the eyes, especially if the planets are near the angles, or either one receives a hard aspect from Mars.

Sun–Mercury

The only aspect which Mercury can make to the Sun is the conjunction, as the furthest Mercury can be from the Sun is 28 degrees. Where it is within 8 degrees, it is said it be combust and thereby weakened. This can result in an overly subjective viewpoint which can be troublesome to the health, as these patients may find it difficult to stand back far enough to take an objective look at the situation and see the part they play in contributing to their own illness.

Where Mercury is at the heart of the Sun, that is, within 17 minutes of orb, it is cazimi. This can give a brilliant mind, with exceptional insight and penetration. The nervous system is likely to be healthy. The combination of the Sun and Mercury corresponds to the puberty of the male and to the vitality of the nervous system. There seems to be a connection with the formation of granulation tissue, which is found in the stage of tissue repair following damage caused by inflammation.

Sun–Venus

As Venus is never more than 48 degrees away from the Sun, the only aspects it can make are the conjunction, semi-sextile and semi-square. Each of these can take the edge off the body's vitality by giving a desire for soft living, good food and general self-indulgence. Unless the aspect is afflicted and the tendency underlined by other chart factors, this is unlikely to be serious. The combination affects glandular tissue and especially the Graafian follicles of the ovary, which are the mature eggs just before they are released on ovulation.

Sun–Mars

Mars in hard aspect to the Sun gives a fast metabolism. Often the person gives off so much heat that they are hot to the touch, but have a subjective feeling of chill and do not like the cold. There is a tendency to acidosis, and it is important to ensure that the organs of elimination are functioning well so that the rapidly produced metabolic wastes are removed promptly from the body. It may be helpful to eat frequent small meals to compensate for all this expenditure of energy.

Even hard aspects between Mars and the Sun can be helpful in warding off illness, as Mars produces the necessary action and heat to overcome invasion of the body's boundaries, as well as deal with internal 'enemies'. Children with these aspects can suddenly run very high fevers, which is an excellent sign that the body's defence system is working well; the process should certainly not be interfered with by giving drugs unless the temperature becomes dangerously high.

The Sun–Mars combination refers to the inflammatory response, and the muscular activity which leads to heat production. Reinhold Ebertin suggests that it has a connection with sperm.

Sun–Jupiter

The Sun and Jupiter in good aspect is a plus point when considering convalescence and the restoration of health, owing to Jupiter's connection with protection and the liver function. It is also a sign of 'healthy blood'.

With the difficult aspects there may be a tendency to over-indulgence, which can be hard on the liver and lead to all the repercussions associated with an immoderate appetite.

Sun–Saturn

Sun–Saturn aspects slow down the metabolism. People with these aspects tend to be cool to the touch, but subjectively feel warm, as they are not losing heat in the same way as those with hard aspects between the Sun and Mars. They can usually tolerate the cold quite well; indeed it can act as a useful stimulant. They may have a poor appetite and be better off with large meals taken at infrequent intervals, if other factors in the chart support this. There is a tendency to alkalinity of the system.

Saturn damps down the vitality of the Sun, so that although there are often few or no episodes of acute illness, neither is there a glowing feeling of health. Later in life the repeated onslaughts on the Sun's vitality can result in chronic, hard-to-resolve conditions. Regular cold water treatments, like a daily cold shower, are beneficial in Sun–Saturn conditions.

The accumulation of mineral deposits in the body tissues and structures is associated with hard Sun–Saturn aspects. This causes the tissues to harden, thicken and lose their flexibility. The conditions include rheumatic problems and arteriosclerosis, in which there are degenerative changes in the arteries. These vessels lose their elasticity, become thicker and often contain deposits of calcium, which, being the main constituent of bone, is the mineral of Saturn. There may also be a connection with hereditary disease. The ageing process also belongs to Sun–Saturn.

Sun–Uranus

Sun–Uranus is associated with the rhythmic functions of the body, such as the heartbeat, pulse and breathing. Where there are difficult aspects this may result in cerebral embolism or effort syndrome, known as neuro-circulatory asthenia (NCA) in the USA. One common cause of cerebral embolism is atrial fibrillation, or disturbed rhythm of the atria of the heart, which fits well with the symbolism of the two planets. NCA is a form of anxiety neurosis where there is no evidence of organic disease and the symptoms and signs resemble a functional disorder of the autonomic nervous system.

There is also a suggestion that even easy aspects between the Sun and Uranus can be linked with paralysis, if other factors support this.

Sun–Neptune

With Sun and Neptune contacts the vitality and immune resistance tend to be low, unless shored up by other positive factors. Anaemia may be one result. There can be disturbances and even breaks in awareness or consciousness. I have one patient with a Sun–Neptune opposition across the sixth-twelfth house axis who has several times been found, or has come to, miles from home. Once she drove her car on to the platform of a major Scottish station, left it there with the keys still in the ignition, boarded the first train and was found by a policeman wandering the streets of London with no recollection of how she got there. On a couple of other occasions when a similar thing happened, alcohol, whose effects are distinctly Neptunian, played a part.

Eye diseases, either of indeterminate origin or to do with the ability to focus, are linked with Neptune aspects to both the Sun and the Moon. Traditionally the Sun rules the right eye of a man and the left eye of a woman, while the Moon rules the right eye of a woman and the left eye of a man. It would be interesting to carry out research to validate this.

Sun–Neptune, as is also the case with Moon–Neptune, can be linked with oedema and disturbed fluid balance in the cells, but the effects are much more pronounced with the Moon, especially in women.

Sun–Pluto

Like Sun–Mars aspects, Sun–Pluto links, even if they are hard, give toughness and resilience to the constitution. The only problem is that if the aspect comes under too much stress for a prolonged period, the organism may be pushed beyond its breaking point. Pluto trining or sextiling the Sun is an excellent sign of regenerative abilities. With the hard aspects there may be a tendency to swellings, tumours and abscess formation. According to Davidson, where Pluto is in a fixed sign afflicting a fixed sign Sun, there is a tendency to sarcoma. However, there would have to be several other very strong significators to back this up.

Sun–Ascendant

The Sun in aspect to the ascendant deals with conscious perceptions of the environment via the organs of sense, especially the eyes. Even a seemingly harmless transit of the Sun to the Ascendant can trigger off latent eye trouble in susceptible individuals.

Sun–Midheaven

This aspect deals with body image and the sense of self. If the Sun and Midheaven are not in harmony there is an unhappy perception of self, which may produce the sense of inadequacy and negative self-image that leads to lowered resistance and susceptibility to illness. This is a general background feature which may provide a breeding ground for health problems, rather than an indication of any specific disorder.

Moon–Mercury

Hard aspects between the Moon and Mercury can produce a mental disposition prone to emotional upset and worry. The specific type of emotion and worry will be indicated by the sign and house placements of the two planets. The mind is strongly conditioned by attitudes picked up in early childhood. Where these attitudes are negative they can sap the strength of the nervous system, both physically and psychologically.

There may be a poor or unreliable memory, or mental or respiratory disorders. Reinhold Ebertin links this aspect with puberty in the female, and with the cerebral and cerebro-spinal fluids.

Moon–Venus

As might be expected, problems with Moon–Venus contacts are more likely to show up in women rather than men. Both planets influence conception and the menstrual cycle, the Moon in its rhythm and ebb and flow of body fluids, and Venus with hormonal secretion and regulation. Where there is an imbalance, there may be a slackness of tone in the menstrual and reproductive function, giving such problems as vaginal discharge, swollen breasts and many of the symptoms of the pre-menstrual syndrome. Easy aspects and the conjunction, especially in Cancer, and to a lesser extent in the other water signs and Taurus, predispose to easy conception, even outside the ovulation period. Adequate contraceptive measures must be taken at all times if the woman does not wish to become pregnant.

Moon–Mars

Moon–Mars represents the mobilization of emotions. An everyday example of this is blushing. In his book *The Astrological Aspects*, Charles Carter states that individuals with inharmonious Moon–Mars aspects may be either self-willed and pugnacious or, if they are 'nice' people, prone to ill-health. Where Moon–Mars emotion does not find a suitable outlet externally – and it does not have to be expressed as anger – it will turn in on itself, thus undermining the health. One survey of patients who survived cancer showed that the common factor was that they had all learned to express their aggression during the time of healing.

It may upset some commonly held, sentimental notions about the nature of health to associate it so strongly with aspects of Mars and Pluto, both of which embody some pretty selfish and ruthless energies. But one law of nature is the survival of the fittest, and that involves quite a degree of competitiveness and self-interest.

Moon–Mars is often associated with copious menstruation, bilious nausea, and fevers which produce reddish skin eruptions.

Reinhold Ebertin links the combination with involuntary muscle movement, thyroid gland function, and Graves' disease. This is a disease which often runs in families, whose cause is unknown. It most commonly affects women and involves increased growth and activity of the thyroid gland, accompanied by protruding eyes, excessive sweating, nervousness and palpitations.

Moon–Jupiter

Classically, hard aspects between the Moon and Jupiter point to a sweet tooth and gluttony, neither of which does wonders for health!

As with Moon–Venus, the emphasis is on slackness of tone, but this time the digestion is likely to be involved. Moon–Jupiter combinations refer to secretions of the liver, pancreas and gall-bladder. Before food can be assimilated (a Moon function), it needs to be broken down into simpler units. Before this breakdown process takes place, fats, which are ruled by Jupiter, need to be emulsified by the bile which is produced in the liver (also ruled by Jupiter) and stored in the gall-bladder. The bile salts are also responsible for ferrying the digested fat products to the wall of the intestine, where they are absorbed. Thus it is not difficult to see that a Moon–Jupiter imbalance can lead to digestive problems, often those involving the gall-bladder and fat metabolism.

Moon–Saturn

Like Sun–Saturn, Moon–Saturn afflictions can show up as hereditary diseases, but the most common pathology is neurosis and depression owing to the fear and abnormal sensitivity Saturn produces when aspecting the Moon. It gives a slowed and inhibited emotional response, which provides a fertile ground for illness of all kinds. It is associated with chronic disturbances in the water balance, defects of mucous membranes and bladder diseases.

Moon–Uranus

Psychologically this aspect is associated with excessive self-will and even perversity. There is often intense emotional excitement, which is greatest in the fire signs. This is combined with sensitivity, a highly strung nature and nervous tension. There can be erratic and overwhelming

ing emotional outbursts. The resulting high-tension, emotional 'electricity' needs to be grounded, and the person soothed and centred by periods of quiet and relaxation in which the charged feelings can be processed and assimilated. Otherwise it is possible that a breakdown in health might occur due to the prolonged over-stimulation of the nervous system.

There can be menstrual irregularities, ovulatory pain and dysmenorrhoea. It can lead to colic in any fluid-excreting organ, such as the bladder and prostate gland, and to disturbances in blood pressure.

Moon–Neptune

Neptune seeks to erode barriers wherever it is found, and here it is emotional separateness which is affected. These people are extremely impressionable and often have difficulty in distinguishing between their own emotions and those of people around them. In some cases this can lead to emotional dependency on others, to the point of being parasitic. Psychosomatic conditions are common, and in extreme cases there can be psychosis and delusional insanity. One problem that may arise is addiction, usually to drugs or alcohol, those substances which further break down barriers and give a sense of oneness with the whole of creation.

As the contact gives dissatisfaction with the inevitable disappointments and restrictions of life in the flesh, and a tendency to give up and retreat from harsh reality, it is detrimental to the fighting spirit needed to shake off illness. Any treatment which keeps Neptune usefully occupied at such a time, for example creative visualization techniques, prayer and meditation, can be powerful tools in turning victim into victor.

The most common physical manifestation which I have found is water retention, generally aggravated by emotional tension, ranging from pre-menstrual bloating to full-blown idiopathic oedema. The latter is a condition of unknown origin whose symptoms are similar to many glandular disturbances, but where the clinical tests all prove negative. Typically, patients have several vague or conflicting diagnoses, depending on how many doctors they have visited. It may be linked with disturbances in osmotic pressure. The distribution of body fluid

can shift dramatically within a few hours or sometimes minutes, especially after exercise and eating even small quantities of food. Clothes
which are loose-fitting when put on in the morning cut into the body by
evening. One patient claimed that she had fasted for five days and drank
nothing but sugarless tea, but had still managed to gain four pounds. I
should add that I have no proof of this either way, and it could be an
alternative manifestation of Moon–Neptune imagination, although that
may be unfair to the patient. That is the problem with Neptune – it is
difficult to distinguish reality from illusion, if in fact there is any such
thing as reality.

I have found that, in many cases, Moon–Neptune trines, even more
than the hard aspects, are linked with food and environmental sen-
sitivities and with asthma.

Moon–Pluto

Reinhold Ebertin links the Moon and Pluto with blood diseases and
hereditary schizophrenia. The most common problems that I have
found are fibroids and excessive menstrual bleeding. Many patients with
the conjunction or hard aspects have either had or been threatened with
a hysterectomy. There is also a link with disturbances of bowel function
and surgical removal of parts of the colon.

During treatment some patients have started to acknowledge an
uncanny degree of intuitive insight and power that they had been afraid
to look at before because they felt overwhelmed by it. With astrological
counselling, and the realization that they were not mad or bad, the
physical problems lessened and became more manageable once the
psychological element was recognized.

Moon–Ascendant

Moon–Ascendant contacts increase subjectivity, causing these people to
take impressions and stimuli from the outside world personally and
very much to heart. Where the aspect is a hard one, or a conjunction,
they may be so strongly attuned to their own particular needs in a given
situation that they are unable to see what, objectively, the appropriate
response might be.

The most common health problem I have found is pre-menstrual syndrome, where the women involved, in the week before menstruation, retain fluid to such an extent that it can alter their appearance and negatively influence their self-image. They crave comforting junk foods, which exacerbates the problem, and find themselves subjected to almost uncontrollable mood changes that contrast strongly with their normal personalities.

Moon–Midheaven

This is said to represent the distribution of blood and other fluid in the body. When a hard Moon–Midheaven aspect is triggered there may be a shift in the distribution of body fluid. The most extreme case is in shock, where the person collapses because a vital organ has been left with an insufficient supply of blood. It has been linked with postural hypotension, where the blood supply to the head diminishes when the person stands up.

Mercury–Venus

The only aspects that can be formed are the conjunction, semi-sextile, semi-square and sextile, which are unlikely to cause trouble unless either planet is afflicted natally by other planets or by transits of the heavier planets. Mercury–Venus relates to the nerve supply of the endocrine glands.

Mercury–Mars

This combination relates to the motor nerves which control the muscles. In hard aspect, there can be spastic paralysis, increased reflex action, irritability of the nerves leading to involuntary twitchings and tics, and inflammation of nervous tissue. In extreme cases there may even be tumours of the nervous tissue. It is a very excitable aspect, often combined with fear and nervousness, and sometimes linked with bilious diarrhoea and thirst.

Mercury–Jupiter

The effect of any stimulus to Mercury-ruled structures or processes will be magnified by this aspect. For example, coffee, tea, cola drinks and food additives, which have an irritant effect on the nervous system, are often badly tolerated by those with hard aspects between Mercury and Jupiter. In turn these substances may not be processed adequately by the liver, leading to systemic nervous disturbances.

Mercury–Saturn

Where Mercury and Saturn are in hard aspect there can be an under-functioning of the nervous system generally, but especially that part supplying the organs of speech and hearing. It is commonly found in cases of dyslexia and deafness. It also refers to the nerve supply to the skeletal system, and afflictions may be linked with stiffness and deep dull pain in the joints.

Mercury–Uranus

Hard aspects between Mercury and Uranus can give a brilliant mind, but one which at times is as easily curbed as a blaze in a fireworks factory. People with these aspects tend to rush about, suffering from a chronic lack of time, and consequently never take the oppor-tunity to relax properly. Periods of low-stimulus rest are essential for them. They need time to contemplate and assimilate all the new and exciting information they have acquired. This is generally the last thing they do, and it tends to take its toll if not dealt with in time.

Physically it refers to the co-ordination of movement and balance, which are monitored by the proprioceptors in the muscles and joints. These respond to changes in joint position, muscle stretch and tendon tension. With this feedback information the muscular system can be orchestrated to function smoothly.

Mercury–Neptune

Problems associated with this aspect are weak nerves, irrational fears, nerve paralysis, loss of consciousness and a decreased ability to feel or sense. It is usually found with a fantasy-rich imagination, which could be better occupied in working with guided imagery or other suitable Neptunian techniques instead of being allowed to worry and undermine confidence.

Mercury–Pluto

Psychologically, people with hard Mercury–Pluto aspects are highly attuned to detecting possible threats to themselves from the words and communications of others. At the slightest hint of perceived danger they may lash out verbally, with unnecessary vehemence. Unnecessary, that is, to the casual observer. For the Mercury–Pluto person it is a survival issue. Their verbal darts are aimed to destroy, and they seldom miss as they have an uncanny perception of their opponent's vulnerability. They often fear that their mind is giving way and that they are heading towards insanity. Patients with this problem can be greatly helped when they start to investigate the meaning of Pluto, but the subject can only be broached when trust has been established, as it is a matter which they guard jealously.

Mercury–Pluto also applies to nervous over-stimulation, the metabolism of the nervous system, and the formation of new nervous tissue.

Mercury–Ascendant

Mercury–Ascendant aspects concern the point at which stimuli from the environment are picked up by the sensory receptors. They relate to the perception of the environment, the nature of which can be seen from the signs, aspects and house placement of Mercury.

Mercury–Midheaven

Reinhold Ebertin relates this combination to the motor-nerve centres of the brain.

Venus–Mars

Hard aspects between Venus and Mars are generally found where there is a plentiful outpouring of sex hormones and consequently a strong sex drive. There may be kidney infections, copious urine, menstrual problems, and possibly a tendency to varicose veins, phlebitis and thrombophlebitis.

Venus–Jupiter

Hard aspects between these planets give a tendency to self-indulgence where food and drink are concerned, coupled with a liver which may not be capable of handling such richness, so that the person tends to run to fat. There may be excessive glandular secretions, especially of the female sex hormones, leading, in men, to some degree of softness. These people are often disinclined to take exercise, which does not help the tendency of this aspect to produce venous engorgement and stasis.

Venus–Saturn

People with these aspects find it difficult to relate spontaneously and easily. Since a feeling of social relatedness ranks high in the list of preventative measures against illness, for this reason alone hard aspects between Venus and Saturn must be reckoned a health hazard.

There may be some malfunction in the secretion of hormones and a slow-down or under-functioning of their regulatory system. Some glands may atrophy or enlarge to try to compensate for the low hormonal output, as, for example, in goitre. This aspect has also been linked with emphysema, where the air sacs of the lungs become distended. There may be under-functioning of the kidneys or hardening of the kidney tubules or glomeruli.

Venus conjunct Saturn in Aquarius has been linked with varicose veins.

Venus–Uranus

Venus–Uranus in hard aspect can give a disturbed rhythm to the sex drive. At one moment there is a great upsurge of sex hormones and a strong urge to relate, the next moment it is gone – nothing there. Now you see it, now you don't. There is general instability throughout the hormonal system and a lack of balance. It is sometimes associated with spasmodic kidney pains.

Where Venus is in a fixed sign in hard aspect to Uranus, there may be a heart murmur.

Venus–Neptune

There may be weakened glandular function and weakness of the sex organs. Some glands may become enlarged, develop diffuse boundaries and release hormones when they are not required. These people may escape into alcoholism or drug abuse. Interestingly, among chronic alcoholics, there is an increase in chronic pancreatitis, in which enzymes leak out of the pancreas to destroy the surrounding tissues.

Relationships and sexuality may be areas of confusion for these people, who are often easily seduced because of a deep longing to merge with an idealized beloved. There may therefore be difficulty in distinguishing their own desires, needs and boundaries from those of anyone with whom they are in intimate contact.

Venus–Pluto

Hard aspects between Venus and Pluto can cause a powerful, sometimes compulsive, sex drive and intense, even destructive, emotions. Glandular secretions are excessive. It is connected with the onset of menstruation and the ovarian function, especially ovulation.

Venus–Ascendant

As this aspect is more concerned with appearance and the complexion, it does not generally have any significant effects on health.

Venus–Midheaven

Reinhold Ebertin links this combination with the third ventricle of the brain and the pituitary, the body's master gland.

Mars–Jupiter

Even with the hard aspects there is no great health risk. Mars–Jupiter gives a rich blood supply, sometimes to the point of engorgement, enlarged organs, and a great capacity to fight off anything which threatens the body's integrity. Davidson says that it is almost a guarantee of immunity.

It can also have a connection with the benign fatty tumours called lipomas.

Mars–Saturn

This combination refers to the processes of bone formation. The classic manifestation of the hard aspects is inflammation of the joints, as in arthritis. There can also be bone malformations, inflammation of the bones or bone marrow, pathological fractures, or paralysis of the muscles of breathing leading to suffocation. Depending on which planet is the stronger, there will be either inflammation or stiffness. It is also linked with gall-stones.

Mars–Uranus

Mars–Uranus is concerned with muscle rhythm, both in muscles like those of the heart and gut, and those under voluntary control like the large muscles used in locomotion. When the process is disrupted, there can be pains and cramps from sudden muscular spasm, or ruptures and wounds. These people usually carry scars from one or more accidents caused by impulsive action or lack of co-ordination. There can also be muscular tics and twitches.

Mars–Neptune

This has been called *the* pathological aspect because Mars, the warrior of the body's defences, is enmeshed in Neptune's invisible net. The body does not know whether to attack or to surrender and while it is paralysed, trying to make up its mind, infection sets up home at whichever site provides the best feeding ground.

There can be paralysis, weakness or wasting of the muscles, and a great susceptibility to infection, with discharge of pus.

Mars–Pluto

With the hard aspects there can be intense inflammations or violent release of toxins. Mars–Pluto has also been linked with parasitic infections, poisonous insect bites, and the bites of wild or large animals. Because these people have a tendency to push themselves to the limits of endurance, there is danger of damage to the muscles and tendons.

Sometimes this aspect is involved with surgery where the natural body parts are replaced; examples are false teeth, replacement joints, artificial limbs and organ transplants.

Mars–Ascendant

This has been linked with surgical operations and accidents, especially burns.

Mars–Midheaven

Reinhold Ebertin relates this aspect to the regulation of body temperature, fever and the functions of the muscles under voluntary control.

Jupiter–Saturn

This combination is connected with under-functioning of the liver, which may also be smaller than normal. The metabolism is slowed down and there is a tendency to gall-bladder and liver problems, including cirrhosis of the liver.

As Saturn restricts Jupiter's protective function, it can be associated with chronic diseases. There can be hardening of the arteries, associated with high blood pressure.

Jupiter–Uranus

There is a tendency to gall-bladder colic, and colics throughout the whole of the gastro-intestinal tract, but these pains do not generally last long. The metabolism is erratic and there can be fatty diarrhoea at times, followed by constipation.

Jupiter–Neptune

If in hard aspect, there is a general lack of tone in the organs of the body. There is a tendency to haemolysis. Because the walls of the small arteries may be more permeable than normal, fluid can leak out, producing waterlogged tissues.

The metabolism is also weak, so that food particles are not broken down properly. This results in fermentation, gas production, and a build-up of gas in the gut leading to abdominal distension. Wrong diagnoses are common as these problems are often of psychological origin.

Jupiter–Pluto

Where these planets are in good aspect it is an excellent sign of ease of recovery and recuperation after illness. Blood transfusions are generally successful and organs regenerate well after injury.

The hard aspects sometimes tend to be associated with compulsive eating and excessive weight gain.

Jupiter–Ascendant

The hard aspects and conjunctions often lead to corpulence, especially in middle age.

Saturn–Uranus

As Uranus represents the pulse of life and Saturn the densest form of matter, lack of alignment between the two can give a tendency to tears or breaks in the hard tissues of the body, such as the bones, joints, skin and teeth. There can be sudden skin eruptions, usually due to shock. In extreme cases this aspect has been linked with amputation.

Saturn–Neptune

Since Neptune dissolves boundaries and Saturn is concerned with forming and maintaining them, a combination of these principles is not an easy one, as they are set on opposite courses. Psychologically the hard aspects are linked with anxieties, neuroses, confusion and phobias. There is generally some kind of inferiority complex and feeling of inadequacy, as it is difficult for these people to define who they are in the world; there may also be a martyr complex. All of this makes a splendid breeding ground for ill-health.

Physically there is a tendency to degeneration of the structural tissues. Examples of this are osteoporosis and osteomalacia. Once illness has set in, it is difficult to shake it off, and there is a tendency to retain metabolic wastes, which of course aggravates any underlying problem.

Saturn–Pluto

Anything which Pluto touches is affected by its intensity. Here the task of Saturn to lay down and maintain solid body structures is intensified, so that there is a tendency to hardening or calcification of connective tissue and bone. There may also be under-development of some organs, because both Saturn and Pluto are energies that concentrate into small spaces. Waste products may not be eliminated, which can lead to potentially serious auto-intoxication (self-poisoning).

Psychologically these people can suffer from severe depression.

Saturn–Ascendant

This aspect can give rise to skin troubles as both principles are concerned with interfaces – Saturn with body boundaries, and the Ascendant with the individual and the environment. In some cases there are chronic middle-ear problems or hereditary short-sightedness.

Saturn–Midheaven

With Saturn in hard aspect to the Midheaven it is difficult for the individual to have a spontaneous and joyous sense of self. It can be linked with disintegration of the personality and ego-related mental disorders. There is a general feeling of being out of sorts.

Uranus–Neptune

As with all aspects between the outer planets, this one will go unnoticed in most charts unless it is sensitively placed. Hard aspects can lead to paralysis or weakness of the rhythmic processes of the body. Examples include breathing disorders, heart failure and stroke. There is a tendency to over-sensitivity and over-reaction. The areas affected will depend on aspects to other planets and the house positions occupied by Uranus and Neptune.

Uranus–Pluto

With Uranus and Pluto in hard aspect and sensitively placed in the chart, or triggered by transit or progression, there can be excessive tone in the body areas represented by the sign and house position of the planets (especially Uranus). This can lead to intense, painful spasms, and possibly changes in some of the biological rhythms of the body.

Uranus–Ascendant

Here the nervous system responds extremely quickly to environmental stimuli, often too quickly for the messages it is picking up to be processed properly. This aspect can be linked with sensitive skin, headaches and sometimes trigeminal neuralgia. Psychologically, people with these aspects can be infuriatingly unpredictable. It is not that they mean to be unreliable, it is simply that they are so much more open to the constantly changing stimuli that they never seem to stay in one place long enough to consolidate. There is a high degree of nervous strain involved in these aspects, which can lead to a breakdown in health if not channelled in some constructive way.

Uranus–Midheaven

This combination does not seem to have any particularly significant implications for health, apart from the general restlessness which it brings.

Neptune–Pluto

Pluto represents the single-minded determination to survive. Neptune is more interested in the death of the separateness of self. Bring these two principles together and there is conflict. Where hard aspects are highlighted in the chart, the person may lack incentives and even the will to live. The patient simply gives up and either waits patiently to die, or submits to a long and tedious illness, sometimes combining the Neptunian tendency to martyrdom with the Plutonian urge for power in a spectacular display of manipulation through guilt and sweet resignation. In the late 1880s and early 1890s there was a Neptune–Pluto conjunction in Gemini. Small wonder, then, that the character of the powerful invalid-martyr appears with such frequency in Victorian novels.

Neptune–Ascendant

It is difficult for people with these aspects to have a clear sense of reality, or perhaps it is more accurate to say that their idea of reality does not correspond to that generally perceived by others. Physically their senses may deceive them, as in, for example, the feeling of the skin crawling. Some may also be sensitive to or dependent on mood-altering drugs and liquids like alcohol, coffee and tea. A polluted atmosphere may also have a detrimental effect on health.

Neptune–Midheaven

The hard aspects may give rise to mental disturbances and a lack of a clear sense of purpose in life, which may be linked with periodic depression.

Pluto–Ascendant

These aspects give people great tenacity of purpose, which can be very helpful in their determination to find the correct therapy and recover. The physical appearance may alter greatly, the person having apparently undergone a transformation. This is especially associated with Pluto transits over the Ascendant.

Pluto–Midheaven

As with Pluto–Ascendant contacts, this aspect is most closely bound up with the determination to get well and to find the right therapy. This is often psychological in nature and tackles the roots of the problem. However, it may also involve an irreversible treatment like amputation, or a deep cleansing and regeneration programme, like the Gerson therapy.

THE SIGNS AND HOUSES

Aries and the First House

Aries represents the principles of assertive energy and the awakening of the awareness of self through interaction with the environment. It rules the head, including the brain tissue, skull and face. It also rules consciousness.

With the Sun in Aries the temperature rises very quickly, both in response to illness and when the person is exposed to the sun and other sources of heat. Such people are liable to heat- and sunstroke.

Saturn in Aries often gives a small head and poor blood supply to the brain. These people are reputed to benefit from yoga exercises, like headstands.

Taurus and the Second House

Taurus represents the principles of gathering together and building up. When Taurus is afflicted, it tends to tumour formation because of its fixity and aggregating force. It rules the throat, tonsils and voice, as well as the thyroid, the heart through the thyroid centre, and the Eustachian tubes and middle ear.

Gemini and the Third House

Gemini represents the principles of connectedness and relatedness, the perception of sensations, and flexibility. Wherever things join, Gemini is indicated. It also has to do with the picking up, conveyance and transfer of information.

It rules all tubes and nerves in the body as well as the lungs, shoulders, arms and hands. It may have associations with the thymus gland and capillaries.

Cancer and the Fourth House

Cancer is linked with containing, surrounding, protecting and nourishing. It rules all mucous and serous membranes. Davidson suggests that it may be connected with the eyeballs, bone marrow, cheeks, ovaries, and the posterior pituitary gland and its hormones. It may also rule some body fluids like breast milk, digestive juices, saliva and chyme. There is a possible connection with glycogen storage in the liver.

Women with afflictions in Cancer may experience difficulties during pregnancy. In some cases, Saturn in Cancer in hard aspect to Uranus may be linked with multiple sclerosis.

Leo and the Fifth House

Leo rules the vitality, the pouring out of life and power. At its best it seems to radiate with the sense of 'I-am-ness', with the sheer joy of simply being. It rules those parts concerned with radiating vital power, the heart, spine and retina of the eye.

The Sun in Leo gives abundant vitality. Where Mars is in Leo, there is so much heat produced from the vital parts that no more should be added, and heat to the back and heart areas is best avoided.

Virgo and the Sixth House

In natal astrology Virgo is concerned with discrimination and craftsmanship – 'getting it right'. It takes orders and executes them economically and efficiently. It does this by analysing, purifying, splitting into categories, and putting everything in its proper place. In the body, where the correct, unadulterated component is not in the right place at the right time and in the right quantity, there is a breakdown in function, not only of the part, but of the whole, which may be why Virgo and sixth-house afflictions are so devastating to health.

Virgo rules the sympathetic nervous system, the intestines (especially the small intestine), the digestive enzymes, spleen, pancreas, diaphragm and the filtering function of the liver.

According to Davidson, those with a strong positive Virgo emphasis do not tend to suffer from cancer, a disease of aggregation, as the body has the ability to break down and assemble the correct materials in the correct place.

Afflictions to Saturn in Virgo are connected with poor circulation and under-function of the liver, hardening of the liver and biliousness. Hernia of the diaphragm is associated with strong Virgo afflictions.

Libra and the Seventh House

Libra is concerned with balancing and harmonizing. Equilibrium is achieved by increasing that which is too little and decreasing that which is too much, as in the maintenance of the electrolyte balance by the process of filtration through the kidneys. It also helps to maintain a steady body temperature. When the temperature rises, blood is shunted to the vessels nearest the skin surface where it loses heat and cools the body. In cold weather the reverse happens, and blood is withdrawn from the peripheral body areas to conserve heat. It is likely that Libra is also connected with other homoeostatic mechanisms.

Libra rules the kidneys, lumbar region, loins, and the eyes through reflex association with Aries. Afflictions to Mars in Libra can give rise to itchy burning eyes and a tendency to skin eruptions associated with kidney dysfunction. It is also prone to ear infections involving discharge. Saturn in Libra or Aries can give thickening of the kidney tubules, which are then unable to function adequately, leading to renal retention.

Scorpio and the Eighth House

Scorpio deals with the processes of transformation and elimination. It therefore has to do with concentrating and holding on to body wastes until they are changed into a form suitable for excretion. It also rules the reproductive processes, from the transformation of the fertilized egg into foetus to the expulsion of the baby from the body in the birth process.

Scorpio rules the colon and all eliminative channels and body outlets, including the nose and sweat glands. The urinary system from the kidney pelvis to the urethra, including the ureters and bladder, belong to Scorpio, as well as all waste products. It used to be thought that the best time to give laxatives was when the Moon was in Scorpio.

Sagittarius and the Ninth House

Sagittarius is concerned with aiming at the far distance and moving from place to place. Afflictions in Sagittarius tend to show up almost anywhere in the body, as well as in the hips and thighs which the sign traditionally rules. It is also connected with locomotion and the lower spinal cord, the ability of the eye to focus, and the left cerebral hemisphere. An afflicted Mars in Sagittarius tends to sciatica, and, since both are hot, this condition responds best to cold packs.

Sports injuries too, especially riding and driving accidents, are associated with Sagittarius. There is a tendency for these mishaps to be much less serious than they might have been, involving an element of recklessness and lucky escape. A typical example is a man with a Sagittarian Sun who constantly pushed his luck when both driving and riding. He was thrown from his horse only seconds after crossing a high narrow railway bridge famed for the number of suicides committed there. Although he suffered some unpleasant injuries, if he had come off any earlier it would have meant certain death. Another person with Sagittarius rising, when speeding dangerously along a normally busy road, skidded out of control a full 360 degrees in the only few seconds when there was no traffic around in either direction.

Capricorn and the Tenth House

Like its ruler Saturn, Capricorn is concerned with defining limits, with slowing down, cooling and condensing into solid matter. It is also associated with the control and structure of large organizations, which is what the body is. The connection with the skin is easy to see, as it defines the limits of the body, while bone provides the underlying condensed framework of the body's structure. Capricorn's controlling function can be found in its proposed rulership of the anterior pituitary gland. This secretes hormones which have wide-reaching regulatory functions throughout the body.

It is also linked with the joints, gall-bladder, calcium metabolism and anti-peristaltic movement. Due to the last association, it used to be the rule that medicine was never given when the transiting Moon was in Capricorn, as the patient would not be able to keep it down.

Afflictions in or emphases on Capricorn may give rise to arterio-sclerosis due to excess cholesterol. There may also be a tendency to sluggish bile production, leading to poor emulsification of fats and to jaundice.

Aquarius and the Eleventh House

Aquarius embodies the principle of many things working together for the good of the whole. When individual parts function on their own without regard to the larger unit, there is disruption. Without co-ordinated cellular respiration, circulation, or transmission of signals via the pyramidal tract (also linked with Aquarius), the ability of the body to function smoothly is severely compromised.

It rules the lower legs and ankles, blood circulation, the corticospinal tract, the rods and cones of the retina, cellular oxidation, and the heart through reflex association with Leo.

An afflicted Saturn in Aquarius is sometimes associated with cataracts. There can also be constant tiredness due to poor cellular respiration. These people need to be in the fresh air, and cold water treatment is of assistance, as well as a low-starch, low-sugar diet.

An afflicted Mars in Aquarius can often react violently to intravenous injections.

Pisces and the Twelfth House

Pisces is the sign of universality. At first it seems odd that such an all-encompassing sign should be limited to the confines of the feet. They do, however, hold in miniature a reflection of the whole body. This principle is used in reflex zone therapy to restore health by working on disturbed areas of the body through the corresponding zone in the foot. Pisces, like Sagittarius, may be connected with the immune system.

It is associated with the feet and toes, the lymph, and lymphatics, the production of mucus and phlegm, as well as the duodenum and sympathetic nervous system through reflex association with Virgo.

Displacement Activities

Illness can also be a displacement activity to avoid looking at problems in other areas. Physical symptoms can often mask underlying psychological issues. Sometimes useful clues about what is really at the root of the matter can be found by looking at the areas of life represented by the house associated with the part of the body concerned. For example, kidney problems may be a substitute for dealing with partnership difficulties, and lower-back pain can disguise deep resentments in the area of sexuality and power-sharing. Table 2 contains a brief summary of possible connections.

THE QUADRUPLICITIES OR CROSSES

There is a strong link between body areas ruled by signs in opposition and/or square to one another. These links often cannot be explained by orthodox medicine, but they are there nevertheless and are a common feature of well-documented syndromes, for example, eye involvement in kidney disorders. Where there are no obvious clues to the associations, it is often helpful to check if there are planets in the same quadruplicity, and to assess what their contribution might be through reflex association.

The Cardinal Signs

The cardinal signs are those which form the angles of the natural zodiac. They are concerned with initiating, with taking action and confronting problems. Medically they are most closely linked with those parts of the

Table 2. Displacement activities

Body Area	House	Issues
Head	1st	Ego, self-assertion
Throat and neck	2nd	Possessions, values
Arms, hands, nerves	3rd	Neighbours, relatives, transport, communications, learning
Stomach and breasts	4th	Home and family, security
Heart and back	5th	Creativity, children
Intestines	6th	Work, duty, co-workers
Kidneys	7th	Relationships
Colon, sex organs, lower back	8th	Sex, shared possessions, inheritance, power struggles
Hips, thighs	9th	Religion, wanderlust, law, higher education
Skin, knees, bones	10th	Career and reputation
Circulation, legs	11th	Friends, groups, goals and objectives, human fellowship
Feet	12th	Unselfishness, the unconscious

body which are in contact with − and therefore confronting − the outside world, that is, the skin (Capricorn) and the mucous membranes of the digestive tract, from mouth to anus (Cancer). The contents of the lumen of the gut are, after all, only held in the body; they are not part of it and still belong to the exterior environment. There are many conditions which have connections with the gut and show in the skin, for example, allergic eczemas and rosacea.

Aries–Libra form another axis which has to do with the self and the other. Aries is the sign of consciousness and awareness of self through assertive interaction with the environment. It has the overall rulership of all the structures of the head, including the eyes. Libra weighs up and decides what belongs to the body and what does not. By the filtering and homoeostatic action of the kidneys (Libra), that which is needed to maintain the body's electrolyte and water balance is selectively retained and that which is not passes into the ureters (Scorpio) for excretion. Renal failure (Libra) can lead to headache, retinal haemorrhage and loss of vision (Aries). An interesting feature is that renal failure may be associated with the development of resistance to the action of vitamin D and impaired absorption of calcium (Capricorn) from the intestine (Cancer), which brings in the other axis of the cardinal cross.

The Fixed Signs

The fixed signs follow the cardinals, consolidating and holding fast to the initial impulse the latter set in motion. The fixed signs are aggregative, tending to accumulate toxins and to proliferate extra cells. Davidson says that the focus of these signs is the heart. I have certainly found in charts of patients with heart conditions where there has been no Leo or Aquarius involvement, a strong Taurus or Scorpio tenancy.

There are many connections between the throat (Taurus) and the reproductive organs (Scorpio), both in folklore and in medicine. The tone of the voice alters with the hormonal state of the sex organs. For instance, boys' voices break at puberty, and many women singers refuse to perform during menstruation as the timbre of the voice changes at that time. Middle European peasant girls used to tie a silk thread round their necks; when it became tight, due to the swelling of the thyroid gland, they knew they were pregnant.

The parotid glands become swollen in the infectious disease of mumps. In adults the infection can lead to orchitis (inflammation of the testicles) or oophoritis (ovarian inflammation), a clear Taurus–Scorpio link-up.

The connection between the heart and circulation is too obvious to require comment. What may not be immediately so clear is the important role the large muscles of the calves (Aquarius) play in returning blood to the heart (Leo). In addition, the corticospinal tract (Aquarius) is the direct pathway from the motor areas of the brain to the spinal cord (Leo).

The Mutable Signs

The mutable signs are focused on the respiratory and nervous systems. Another term for them is the common signs, which refers to the idea that they are a common ground shared between otherwise quite separate areas or functions.

Gemini is the messenger between the outside world and the body. It collects stimuli from the external and internal environments and passes them on. Sagittarius, its opposite sign, is concerned with processing this information into a meaningful whole. It works out patterns and 'laws' which can be used to understand and advise on the situation should it arise again. Gemini and Sagittarius are both involved in conditions of the lungs and nerves.

The Virgo–Pisces axis concerns service. Virgo has to do with making creative ideas concrete. It rules the sympathetic nervous system and is the link between psyche and soma, mind and body. Where this breaks down, complications arise in the form of psychosomatic disorders.

Virgo is also the sign of purity, especially in dietary matters. Increasingly there is recognition of the links between low-vitality food, psychological disorders and lowered immunity.

Pisces lies at the shoreline of self and not-self. Pisces yearns for union with the greater whole, which is commonly displaced into alcohol and drug abuse. Another manifestation is in the auto-immune diseases, where the body fails to distinguish between self and the aggressor and attacks its own tissues. There is increasing evidence of the tie-up between the quality of food (Virgo) and the integrity or otherwise of the immune system (Pisces) in the work of such pioneers as Dr Max Gerson in his treatment of cancer. Conversely, the work of the Simontons, also with cancer, shows clearly the value of creative visualization (Pisces) in improving the health of the body (Virgo).

The mutable signs have the reputation of being the least robust, probably because of their vital, and therefore vulnerable, role as the body's mediators.

THE ELEMENTS

The elements feature large in Indian philosophy and the two schools of medicine that have grown out of it – Ayurveda, the traditional Indian medicine, and Tibetan medicine. Ingrid Naiman has built a major bridge between Eastern and Western thought in the second volume of her book *The Astrology of Healing*, in which she translates many of the insights of these systems into modern astrological language. This publication, on which much of the following information is based, is highly recommended for a deeper study of the subject than can be provided here.

It is not always easy to judge the relative proportions of the elements in a chart, as it does not depend just on the number of planets in the respective signs, although that is of course important. The element in which the Moon is placed is highly significant. The strengths of those planets associated with a particular element, the house emphasis, as well as the transits, need to be considered. In estimating the element balance you should examine:

1. The element of the Moon
2. The number and qualities of planets in each element
3. The aspects of the planets associated with each element
4. The transits of Mars, Saturn, Uranus, Neptune and Pluto
5. The house emphasis

Transiting planets can affect the natal element balance markedly. Mars increases fire; Saturn and Pluto, earth; Uranus, air; and Neptune, water. The heavier the planet and the longer the transit, the greater the influence will be. In the natal chart, a mutable emphasis will increase the element of air; a cardinal emphasis, the element of fire; and a fixed emphasis, that of water.

In traditional European physiology, diseases were thought to be due to imbalances of the four body fluids or humours. These were blood, phlegm, yellow bile and black bile. People with a preponderance of blood were said to be sanguine, and this is generally associated with the air signs. Yellow bile predominating gave a choleric temperament, associated with fire, while black bile was claimed for the melancholic temperament of earth and phlegm for the phlegmatic water triplicity.

Suggested treatments for element imbalances are to be found in Chapter 7 on materia medica.

Air

The air signs are Gemini, Libra and Aquarius. The third, seventh and eleventh are the air houses, and Mercury and Uranus the air planets. Transits of these planets, and especially Uranus, can increase the air quality of a chart. Uranus is disruptive at the best of times, but in a chart which already has an air overload its transit to a sensitive point can be devastating.

Air is considered to be the most crucial of all the elements, as it activates the potential of all the others. Without it none of the other elements can function.

Air connects. Psychologically it is concerned with connections between people, with equal and fair relationships, and with being in touch with what is happening in the wider world.

In the body it rules anything which connects, for example, tubes, ducts, nerves, speech, touch, co-ordination and propulsion of any kind. The air element does not rule the physical organs as such, but rather the principle of movement through them, the function of connectedness. For example, it rules peristalsis, bowel movements, sneezing, urination and the inflow and outflow of breath. This is a clear connection with the principle of Uranus.

The air element becomes prominent with age and is also strong between 2 a.m. and 6 a.m. People with excess air function often wake up in the early hours of the morning and find it difficult, if not impossible to get back to sleep, although they have had no difficulty in falling asleep earlier in the evening.

Air qualities can be increased by dry and windy weather. Excess sunlight, X-rays, computer and television radiation, and shock and fear also have an exacerbating effect, not to mention the constant barrage of information and stimuli from the media.

An excess of air in a person can be checked by examining their appearance, digestion, movements and mental activity.

1. Appearance

These people have bodies which are lean and dry, both internally and externally. Although they can be youthful in nature, their skin and appearance ages more quickly than normal.

2. Digestion

The digestion is poor and the appetite comes and goes. These people need to eat little and often, and they are frequently thirsty. There is a tendency to low blood sugar, flatulence and constipation. Excess air tends to accumulate in the lower abdomen. A pronounced and pro- longed excess of air can lead to serious ageing diseases, senility, convulsions, epilepsy, and even paralysis and insanity.

3. Movements

The movements are quick and nimble. These people burn up too much energy because of their excessive response to stimuli. Their joints creak and they are prone to shooting pains and muscle twitches.

4. Mental activity

The mind never switches off. Such people even tend to talk in their sleep in the early hours of the morning. They are highly strung and find it difficult to relax. They jump from one source of stimuli to another without much self-control, and they hate to be alone. They are the type, according to Ingrid Naiman, who cannot even go to the bathroom without a book or radio, and preferably both! Although they are very quick at picking up information, they do not process and integrate it well, so that the long-term memory is poor. Nothing goes deep, and they are prone to fretting, worrying and anxiety, which leads to fear- fulness. They lack groundedness and the ability to anchor and use all the information they acquire.

The image for excess air is of a skinny, nervy trend-chaser, rushing from one fashionable scene to the next, whether it be in clothes, art, literature, or the workshops of the latest guru of health or spirituality. The urge is to be where it is all happening. He or she lives on coffee, lettuce leaves and first nights. Ingrid Naiman is of the opinion that A I D S is an excess air condition.

Fire

The fire signs are Aries, Leo and Sagittarius and the fire houses the first, fifth and ninth. The Sun, Mars and Jupiter are the fire planets.

Fire rules transformation and sight, both physical and psychological. It therefore regulates the process of internal combustion, that is, digestion, the production of insulin, body temperature, and the elimination of toxins and waste products. It rules the immune system, which is concerned with fighting off foreign bodies. Fire is competitive and idealistic, with a strong sense of fair play, but it is also very vulnerable and easily threatened by the other elements. It is predominant from puberty to middle age and strong at noon, in summer and after eating, when the digestive processes are activated.

The balance of fire in a person is assessed by examining the urine, skin colour, eyes, digestion, emotions and resistance to disease.

1. The Urine

Where the urine is of a light colour, fire is low. Fire rules the digestive processes, and pale urine generally shows low excretion of waste products. When the urine is dark and smelly, fire is high.

2. The Skin

A rosy to red complexion shows normal to high fire. Where fire is high, there is a tendency towards the greasy, teenage-type skin problems and pimples. The skin is prone to inflammations and the body odour is strong. Heat is poorly tolerated because the body is producing so much of its own. A pale skin that is cold and has little oil indicates low fire.

3. The Eyes

Bright healthy eyes show normal fire. Dull eyes and short-sightedness indicate low fire. Long-sightedness is a sign of excess fire.

4. The Digestion

Excess fire shows up in a voracious appetite, where the person is hungry again soon after eating. It can be associated with thirst and diarrhoea, and in severe cases with jaundice and hepatitis. Low fire gives poor digestion. Partially digested food begins to ferment, leading to the formation of gas, which in turn gives rise to confusion and headaches. Most headaches, according to Ingrid Naiman, are due to low fire. Diabetes is also associated with low fire.

5. The Emotions

A good balance of fire gives cheerfulness, optimism and spontaneity. There is a strong enthusiasm for causes. Fire is always vulnerable and hates to have its weaknesses exposed. Where it is high, provoke it at your peril! Excess fire leads to anger, irritability and aggression, both against others and self. When fire is low, so is self-esteem, drive, confidence, any sense of well-being and vision for the future. Fire is what produces happiness, and lack of fire gives depression and an unwillingness to face up to life's challenges.

6. Immunity

Fire is competitive. A good balance of fire gives the ability to resist infection by what the body regards as foreign and dangerous invaders. Excess fire over-reacts with high temperatures and inflammations. Low fire means poor defences and consequently increased susceptibility to disease.

The image of excess fire is of an irascible and apoplectic retired Indian Army colonel with gout. The curries he eats are as fiery as his temper. He loves his tipple and can work himself into a frenzy tub-thumping about his latest crackpot (according to his neighbours) crusade, usually concerning some esoteric philosophy.

Fire qualities are damped down by discouraging competition and by the sense of fair play. Fire becomes erratic with excess alcohol and excitement.

Water

The water signs are Cancer, Scorpio and Pisces and its houses are the fourth, eighth and twelfth. The water planets are the Moon, Venus and Neptune, and possibly Jupiter when it is afflicted. Water is most active in childhood, which is why catarrhal complaints are so common then.

Water is the provider, both socially and physically, of cohesion. The quality of this relatedness falls somewhere between the stimulating, but superficial, light touch of air and the solid, unyielding attachment of earth. It flows into all interstices, lubricating and connecting. Water rules the lymphatic circulation and all body fluids; it is anabolic, that is, it builds up, unlike fire which breaks down through digestion. It is also associated with taste in all senses of the word, including the physical ability to distinguish flavour as well as the perception of good and bad taste in relation to both behaviour and aesthetics.

1. Body type

There is a voluptuousness about the water type. The body is smooth, plump and soft, and the movements slow, flowing and graceful. The hair is thick and plentiful, the eyes soft and melting. The sex drive is strong and the body temperature low. Where there is excess water it can lead to overweight and laziness, but the weight is not due to fat; the body is simply waterlogged. Davidson suggests that over-watery people benefit from living by the sea and breathing salt air. This draws the water, by osmosis, out of the lungs and into the bronchial tree, where it can be coughed up and removed from the body.

2. Voice

The water type speaks in a monotone, and one sentence runs into another without punctuation.

3. Personality

When water is balanced the person is calm and unruffled. Its great gift is that of serenity. Water has an urgent need to protect itself and its own against the outside world, so when there is an excess or imbalance of water it can lead to greed, clinginess and possessiveness caused by insecurity. Everything is seen and valued subjectively, and this may be quite at odds with external reality and other people's view of what is taking place. It is hard for water to be objective. The memory is retentive, which contrasts strongly with air which rules short-term memory.

The image of excess water is that of a plump and luscious harem lady lolling indolently on cushions, indulging herself with sweetmeats, waiting to be summoned to the royal bedchamber. She is dreaming up schemes whereby she and her offspring, sired by the sultan, can survive the intrigues swirling around her.

Where water is low it is rather like excess air and is treated in the same way. The person is stiff, dehydrated and has difficulties in sleeping. There is a lack of softness and calmness.

Earth

The earth signs are Taurus, Virgo and Capricorn and the houses the second, sixth and tenth. The planets most associated with earth are Saturn and Pluto.

Earth has to do with the formation and laying down of the basic materials for construction, growth, maintenance and repair of body tissues. It is more anabolic, that is, it builds up even more than water. It is associated with the sense of smell, both physically and in the sense of scenting danger. Earth is survival-orientated.

It is strong in children and also in the convalescent, rebuilding stage after illness.

It rules those body parts which are hard and structural, such as the skin, bones, teeth, nails, cartilage and muscle tendons.

1. Body type

Earth is hardy and possesses great stamina. Where it is in excess, all the body tissues become denser. The skin thickens to a leather-like consistency and there is a tendency to sclerosis, calcium deposition, sluggishness and increased body hair.

2. Personality

Earth is materialistic, cautious and respects tradition. It likes to control situations and obey natural laws. It does not care for change or unpredictability and tends to the small-shopkeeper mentality. Where there is excess earth there is a resistance to new ideas of any kind, especially those of a spiritual nature.

The image for excess earth is of a squat and truculent country bumpkin, his skin leathery from exposure to the elements, his mind slow and cunning. He is standing ruminating with a belly full of potatoes, straw in his hair and pitchfork in hand, blocking the entrance to his road against 'them furriners' with their new-fangled notions.

MIDPOINTS

A midpoint is a sensitive point exactly halfway between the shortest distance between two planets. The shorthand method of writing it is, in the case of the Sun and Moon, Sun/Moon. When another planet falls on that midpoint we write, if it is Pluto, Pluto = Sun/Moon, which means that Pluto is situated halfway between the Sun and the Moon. To find the midpoint between two planets convert their positions into zodiacal longitude, add them together and divide by two. There is a table of zodiacal longitudes on page 116.

For example, if the Sun is at 19.52 Taurus and the Moon is at 9.18 Gemini, their midpoint is:

$$
\begin{aligned}
\text{Sun} \quad 19.52 + 30 &= 49.52 \\
\text{Plus} & \\
\text{Moon} \quad 9.18 + 60 &= 69.18 \\
&= 118.70 \\
\text{Divide by 2} \quad &= 59.35 \\
&= 29.35 \text{ Taurus}
\end{aligned}
$$

There is no universal agreement about the orbs used with midpoints. I use one degree. Experts in midpoints, like Charles Harvey and Michael Harding, find that all aspects based on 45 degrees, including the so-called minor semi-square and sesquiquadrate, as well as the conjunction, are important. The Ebertins, who have researched midpoints extensively, have developed the 45-degree dial, an astrological tool which greatly simplifies the identification of all these aspects.

To find the meaning of a planet at any midpoint it is necessary to consider the meaning of the combination of the two planets forming the midpoint, and then work out how the qualities of the third planet at their focal point would affect this combination, or be affected by it. Reinhold Ebertin's *The Combination of Stellar Influences* gives some excellent, if somewhat sparse, information on the interpretation of midpoints. By using keywords, it is possible to gain some insight into how activated midpoints might manifest pathologically. The following keywords are to be taken as guidelines only and can be fleshed out using the information on the planets given above.

Sun – Heart, cell, vitality
Moon – Emotions, body fluids
Mercury – Nervous system
Venus – Glandular system
Mars – Muscles, inflammatory response

Jupiter – Liver
Saturn – Body structure
Uranus – Rhythmic pulsation
Neptune – Dissolution
Pluto – Survival, excretion, regeneration

Some of the most important health midpoints are Sun/Moon, Mars/Neptune, Mars/Saturn and Saturn/Neptune.

The Sun/Moon combination refers to the harmony, or otherwise, between the will and the habitual response. The Moon provides the nourishment that enables the Sun to shine. Any planet at this midpoint, either natally or by transit, will affect this dynamic. For example, Pluto at this midpoint indicates a critical phase where life purpose and direction seem to be torn apart and destroyed, only to be reconstituted in a new and more potent form. The past is left behind for ever, and a new way of expressing and supporting creativity laid down. If this process is resisted, it can lead to a massive breakdown in health. Uranus at this midpoint shows sudden and periodic changes in whatever life rhythms form the status quo at the time. The effect can be disruptive until a new and more valid pattern is established.

Mars, the principle of self-assertion, and Neptune, the urge to dissolve all barriers and to renounce ego-centredness, make uneasy bedfellows. Any planet at their midpoint becomes involved in the conflict between these two quite disparate energies. When the Sun is here, vitality can be low and there is a danger of poor resistance to infection. If Jupiter is at the midpoint, liver function can be weak, or there can be a tendency to lung infections.

Mars/Saturn, where the aspect is easy, refers to the disciplined use of energy; where it is hard, free expression of muscular activity is blocked and frustrated, and the blood and inflammatory response may be inadequate. With Venus at this midpoint there may be glandular dysfunction.

The Saturn/Neptune combination is about forming and maintaining structure versus dissolving it. Mars at the midpoint may be connected with muscle wasting or hardening, low energy or malformed red blood cells.

As with all the other interpretations in this chapter, it is by no means inevitable that the pathological conditions associated with these midpoints will arise. It is fascinating and awe-inspiring to trace the connection of the planets with anatomy, physiology and pathology, but the most desirable function of medical astrology in the healing arts is surely to prevent problems arising in the first place. Suggestions as to how to do this, and also for the appropriate action to take when things have gone wrong, can be found in the last two chapters.

REFERENCES

Carter, Charles, *The Astrological Aspects*, L. N. Fowler & Co., Romford, 1981

Carter, Charles, *The Astrology of Accidents*, Theosophical Publishing House, London, 1931

Daath, Heinrich, *Medical Astrology*, L. N. Fowler & Co., London, 1914

Darling, Dr Harry, *Essentials of Medical Astrology*, American Federation of Astrologers, Tempe, Arizona, 1981

Davidson, Dr William, *Medical Lectures*, Astrological Bureau, Monroe, 1959

Ebertin, Dr Baldur, *Kosmobiologische Diagnostik*, 3 vols, Ebertin Verlag, Freiburg im Breisgau, ud

Ebertin, Reinhold, *The Combination of Stellar Influences*, American Foundation of Astrologers, Monroe, 1972

Gerson, Dr Max, *A Cancer Therapy – Results of Fifty Cases*, Gerson Institute, Bonita, California, 1986

Hand, Robert, *Horoscope Symbols*, Para Research, Rockport, Massachusetts, 1981

Lilly, William, *Christian Astrology*, 1647. Regulus Facsimile Editions, London, 1985

Millard, Dr Margaret, *Casenotes of a Medical Astrologer*, Samuel Weiser, New York, 1980

Naiman, Ingrid, *The Elements*, *The Astrology of Healing* Vol. 2, Seventh Ray Press, Santa Fe, 1986

Simonton, Carl, Matthews-Simonton, Stephanie, and Creighton, James, *Getting Well Again*, Bantam Books, New York, 1981

Watson, Lyall, *Supernature*, Coronet, London, 1973

4

THE DEGREE AREAS

Primarily there is an analogy, a sympathy, a communication, an adelphixis between each zodiacal division and some definite zone of the body. The location of these is broadly but closely defined.

Heinrich Daath *Medical Astrology*

The bulk of the information on the degree areas given below comes from the work of Elsbeth and Reinhold Ebertin which appeared in *Anatomische Entsprechungen der Tierkreisgrade*, and is reproduced by kind permission of the Hermann Bauer Verlag. The translation is my own. Unfortunately, the exact meaning of a few of the terms remains unclear, even after consultation with German medical colleagues. However, from the zodiacal area concerned, it is relatively simple to give a fairly reliable approximation. The doubtful terms are indicated by a question-mark.

The areas and conditions in brackets are those put forward by Charles Carter. Although he did include them along with his own work, Reinhold Ebertin is of the opinion that these degree areas are not as reliable as those he himself uses.

There is some dispute about where one degree ends and another begins. Some insist, for example, that 1 Scorpio runs from 0 to 0 degrees 59 minutes. Others are equally adamant that it starts at 1 Scorpio and continues until 1 degree 59 minutes. The only way to solve the dilemma is to try it out and see which method works best for you.

Those working in the medical field might be interested in checking their suitability for their chosen career according to Carter. He gives as the areas for medical ability 4 degrees Cancer and Capricorn, 18 to 22 degrees Leo and Aquarius, 6 degrees Gemini and Sagittarius, and 22 degrees of the mutable signs. A study carried out by Rupert Gleadon and Brigadier R. Firebrace, quoted by John Addey in *Harmonics in Astrology*, examined the degree of the Sun in the natal charts of 7302 doctors. They found that the peak occurred at 22 degrees Taurus.

The azimene degrees are also included in the list. These degrees, which are sometimes called degrees lame and deficient, come from William Lilly's *Christian Astrology*. He says that blindness, deafness, lameness or any other crippling disability or deformity can often be explained by the person having the Ascendant, the Ascendant ruler, the Moon or the most important planet, in either the natal chart or the decumbiture chart, in any of the azimene degrees.

Dr Margaret Millard, who has done some work on the charts of AIDS sufferers, has suggested that there may be a correspondence between the incidence of AIDS and 16 degrees of the mutable signs, but most especially 16 degrees Sagittarius. However, she adds that a great deal more research must be carried out before regarding this as a certainty. Machon, a Spanish astrologer researching the connections between degree areas and the chromosomes, is also coming up with similar results.

There is no apparent explanation for certain degrees having particular associations. There has simply been an accumulation of empirical and symbolic evidence that this is so. Some of the degree areas have been linked with fixed stars. In *Harmonics in Astrology*, John Addey says that degree-area influences always arise by virtue of the coincidence of certain harmonics, and that some are undoubtedly based on highly complex harmonic combinations. He also makes the point that for every degree area which positively denotes a certain attribute, there is usually a negative degree area which militates against that trait. This and the whole field of harmonics in relation to medical astrology is without doubt going to be one of the major areas of research in the future.

Charles Harvey has conducted what must be one of the finest pieces of research in medical astrology. He looked at all the available charts of the descendants of Queen Victoria who were either carriers (five cases) or sufferers (seven cases) of haemophilia. The most striking factors which he found were that the longitude of Queen Victoria's Saturn and Mars/Saturn midpoint appear to locate specific degree areas which are transmitted from generation to generation. Saturn and the Saturn/Mars midpoint, as well as Jupiter which has traditional associations with the blood, tended to occur in these same degree areas and in areas in an eighth harmonic (45-degree based) relationship to them, in both the charts of the carriers and the sufferers. The significant degrees he found were 28 degrees of the mutables and 8–9 degrees of the cardinals. 13–14 and 22–23 degrees of the fixed signs were also prominent.

Charles Carter, in a footnote to his entry on abscesses in *An Encyclopaedia of Psychological Astrology* and referring to degree areas, underlines the importance of midpoints. He writes: 'In all cases where these special degrees are mentioned in connection with certain character-istics, pathological or otherwise, the student is asked to bear in mind that they may be brought into action by being "bracketed" between two bodies.'

When using the degree areas, the most sensitive points to check are the degrees occupied by the Sun, Moon, Ascendant, Ascendant ruler and the Mars/Neptune and Mars/Saturn midpoints, in both the natal chart and the decumbiture chart, if this is used. Also important are the positions stressed by transits of the heavy planets and the degree of the progressed Sun.

It is often the case that the anatomical structure represented by a specific degree is found to be associated with the degree in opposition, and sometimes with those in square to it. For example, the sex organs generally are ruled by Scorpio but also have a strong connection with Taurus. I have seen so many women with gynaecological problems who also have chronic sore throats that it is almost a surprise not to find the two together. The case notes I have in front of me at the moment show Saturn at 15.50 degrees Taurus. The patient, not unexpectedly, has constant throat trouble but also (see 16 degrees Scorpio) a disturbance in ovarian function.

Aries

1 Cerebrum
2 Midbrain

3 Cerebellum (Abscess)
4 Pineal gland (Goitre)
5 Eye, both right and left (Hair)
6 Eye socket, orbital cavity
7 The ears (Jaundice)
8 Cheekbone
9 Lens of eye
10 Eyeball
11 Optic nerve
12 Tongue (Hair)
13 Ventricles of brain (Rheumatism)
14 Frontal lobes of brain?
15 Lateral lobes of brain? (Suicide, stroke)
16 Pons
17 Vertebral canal
18 Nerve connections – Synapses?
19 Corpus callosum cerebri?
20 Hyoid bone
21 Eye muscles (Abscess)
22 Cheek muscles
23 Muscles of mastication
24 Zygomatic muscle?
25 Sternocleidomastoid muscle
26 Skull
27 Fornix/frontal bone? (Tuberculosis)
28 Fornix/parietal and occipital bones? (Hair)
29 Auditory canal (Bronchitis)
30 Parotid gland

Taurus

0 Throat, gullet
1 Palate
2 Pharynx – oral part
3 Uvula
4 Pharyngeal cavity

5 Larynx
6 Vocal cords. Azimene
7 Cervical nerves. Azimene
8 Jugular veins. Azimene
9 Cervical veins. Azimene. (Alcoholism)
10 Cervical and brachial plexi. Azimene. (Nervous debility)
11 Cervical and brachial plexi
12 Cervical and brachial plexi
13 Cervical and brachial plexi
14 True vocal cords
15 Epiglottis
16 Carotid arteries (Abscess)
17 Thyroid gland and tonsils
18 Lymph vessels (Hair)
19 Maxillary artery
20 Occiput (Goitre)
21 Arteries of nasal cavity
22 Tongue muscles
23 Teeth (Rheumatism)
24 Upper jaw
25 Lower jaw (Alcoholism, adenoids, suicide)
26 Nasal bone
27 Atlas
28 Deltoid muscle and main neck muscles
29 Deltoid muscle and main neck muscles (Eyesight)
30 Trapezius muscle

Gemini

1 Trachea
2 Oesophagus
3 Upper right pulmonary lobe (Appendicitis)
4 Lower right pulmonary lobe
5 Upper left pulmonary lobe
6 Lower left pulmonary lobe (Morbid fears, pneumonia)
7 Apex of lungs (Heart)

8 Bronchi (Eyesight)
9 Pulmonary arteries (Rheumatic fever)
10 Hilum of lungs (Enteric fever)
11 Thymus gland
12 Tracheal mucosa
13 Pulmonary veins (Rheumatic fever)
14 Clavicle
15 Scapulae
16 Pleura
17 First rib
18 Second rib (Chronic glomerulonephritis, asthma)
19 Laryngeal muscles
20 Third rib
21 Arm muscles (Enteric fever)
22 Upper arm (Appendicitis, insanity)
23 Head of the humerus (Spine)
24 Olecranon
25 Radius (Nervous debility)
26 Wrist bones (Suicide)
27 Fingers
28 Metacarpal bones (Tuberculosis)
29 Fourth rib
30 Fifth rib

Cancer

1 Sixth rib
2 Seventh rib
3 Eighth rib (Eyesight)
4 Ninth rib
5 Tenth to twelfth ribs
6 Diaphragm
7 Thoracic cavity
8 Oesophageal opening of diaphragm (Paralysis)
9 Pylorus. Azimene
10 Fundus of stomach. Azimene

11 Gastric veins. Azimene. (Chronic glomerulonephritis)
12 Greater curvature of stomach. Azimene
13 Lesser curvature of stomach. Azimene
14 Stomach walls. Azimene
15 Gastric nerves. Azimene. (Suicide)
16 Pancreas
17 Duodenal opening of pancreatic duct
18 Duodenal opening of pancreatic duct
19 Ampulla of bile duct. Perhaps bile
20 Superior pancreatico-duodenal artery?
21 Inferior pancreatico-duodenal artery?
22 Gastric mucosa
23 Gastric blood vessels
24 Blood vessels of digestive organs
25 Blood vessels of digestive organs
26 Mammary glands
27 Nipples
28 Cartilage of ribs (Hair)
29 Spleen (Bronchitis)
30 Twelfth thoracic vertebra

Leo

1 Left coronary artery
2 Aorta
3 Right coronary artery
4 Left carotid artery
5 Right carotid artery (Hair)
6 Entrance of pulmonary artery (Eyesight)
7 Left coronary vein
8 Inferior vena cava (Anaemia, hearing)
9 Superior vena cava (Alcoholism)
10 Jugular vein
11 Subclavian veins
12 Vertebral column
13 Right ventricle of heart (Rheumatic fever)

14 Left ventricle of heart
15 Right atrium
16 Left atrium
17 Right auricle
18 Right cardiac cavity. Azimene
19 Ventricular septum (Spine)
20 Mitral valve
21 Left atrium
22 Left auricle (Appendicitis)
23 Left auricle (Rheumatism)
24 Papillary muscles
25 Pericardium (Alcoholism, abscess)
26 Myocardium
27 Chordae tendinae. Azimene. (Goitre)
28 Chordae tendinae. Azimene
29 Atrioventricular septum? (Neuritis)
30 Back

Virgo

1 Duodenum
2 Small intestine
3 Appendix, caecum (Appendicitis)
4 Ascending colon (Asthma)
5 Transverse colon
6 Descending colon
7 Rectum
8 Abdominal cavity
9 Right hepatic lobe (Rheumatic fever)
10 Left hepatic lobe, bile (Enteric fever)
11 Falciform (or coronary?) ligament of liver, bile
12 Abdominal aorta
13 Hepatic arteries
14 Cystic arteries
15 'Bare area' of liver
16 Groove for inferior vena cava

17 Abdominal muscles
18 Obliquus abdominis muscles
19 Oesophageal groove?
20 Bile duct
21 Cystic duct (Enteric fever)
22 Gall-bladder (Insanity, appendicitis)
23 Capsule and ligaments of liver (Spine)
24 Capsule and ligaments of liver
25 Liver (Cancer, gout, arthritis)
26 Abdominal veins (Suicide)
27 Iliac veins (Chronic glomerulonephritis)
28 Hepatic plexus (Tuberculosis)
29 Quadrate lobe of liver
30 Hepatic duct

Libra

1 Renal pelvis
2 Renal cortex
3 Adrenals (Abscess)
4 Kidney surface (Goitre)
5 Renal pyramids
6 Pubis
7 Nerve supply to kidney and renal pelvis (Jaundice)
8 Nerve supply to kidney and renal pelvis
9 Nerve supply to kidney and renal pelvis
10 Nerve supply to kidney and renal pelvis
11 Nerve supply to kidney and renal pelvis
12 Left renal system
13 Right renal system
14 Left inguinal lymph nodes
15 Right inguinal lymph nodes (Suicide, stroke)
16 Renal arteries
17 Suprarenal arteries
18 Fatty capsule of kidneys (Chronic glomerulonephritis)
19 Calyx major

20 Calyx minor
21 Renal hilum
22 Renal veins
23 Suprarenal veins
24 Blood vessels of renal cortex
25 Blood vessels of renal cortex
26 Vascular system of skin
27 Vascular system of skin (Tuberculosis)
28 Bladder (Hair)
29 Right ureter
30 Left ureter

Scorpio

1 Urethra
2 Urethral meatus
3 Prostate, uterus
4 Testicles, right side of uterus
5 Testicles, left side of uterus
6 Right epididymus, uterine cavity
7 Left epididymus, right Fallopian tube
8 Scrotum, left Fallopian tube
9 Sperm duct, vagina (Alcoholism)
10 Corpus cavernosum of penis (Nervous debility)
11 Penis, Labia majora
12 Seminal vesicles
13 Vulva, Labia minora, glans penis (Chronic glomerulonephritis)
14 Foreskin
15 Cowper's glands
16 Right ovary, cochlea of inner ear (Abscess)
17 Testicular lobes, left ovary
18 Vas deferens, hymen (Appendicitis, hair)
19 Uterine ligaments, Haller's net? Azimene
20 Ligaments of penis, Bartholin's glands (Goitre)
21 Sphenoid sinus
22 Ethmoid bone (and ligaments?)

23 Nasal bone, fimbria of Fallopian tubes (Rheumatism)
24 Nasal septum
25 Coccyx, Fallopian tubes (Tonsils, adenoids, alcoholism)
26 Perineum
27 Anus
28 Mucous membranes. Azimene
29 Vomer (Sight)
30 Nasal muscles

Sagittarius

1 Pelvic bones. Azimene
2 Pelvic girdle
3 Ischia (Appendicitis)
4 Femur
5 Right femoral artery* (Hair)
6 Left femoral artery* (Morbid fears, pneumonia)
7 Right superficial femoral artery.* Azimene
8 Left superficial femoral artery.* Azimene
9 Right lymphatic vessels. Eye diseases, as this is the degree of the fixed star Antares (Rheumatic fever)
10 Left lymphatic vessels (Enteric fever)
11 Adductor muscles
12 Long saphenous veins
13 Long saphenous veins (Rheumatic fever)
14 Cutaneous vessels of the thighs
15 Right iliac vein
16 Left iliac vein
17 Sciatic nerve
18 Right femur. Azimene. (Asthma)
19 Left femur. Azimene
20 Head of right femur
21 Head of left femur (Enteric fever)
22 Right trochanter (Insanity, appendicitis)

*It is difficult to determine just which arteries are referred to here. Possibly the femoral, popliteal or profunda femoris vessels. In any case arteries of the thigh are meant.

23 Left trochanter (Spine)
24 Popliteal fossa
25 Condyles of right femur (Nervous debility, gout)
26 Condyles of left femur
27 Gluteal muscles
28 Right leg muscles (Tuberculosis)
29 Left leg muscles
30 Pear-shaped muscle?

Capricorn

1 Right patella
2 Left patella
3 Cutaneous nerves of thigh (Sight)
4 Cutaneous nerves of lower leg
5 Cutaneous nerves of knee
6 Right adductor muscle
7 Left adductor muscle
8 Lymph vessels – of knee? (Paralysis)
9 Nerves of knee
10 Right cruciate ligaments
11 Left cruciate ligaments
12 Right knee joint
13 Left knee joint
14 Right knee cartilage
15 Left knee cartilage
16 Condyle of right tibia
17 Condyle of left tibia
18 Ligaments of right knee
19 Ligaments of left knee
20 Tendons of right knee
21 Tendons of left knee
22 Muscle insertions of upper to lower legs
23 Muscle insertions of upper to lower legs
24 Muscle insertions of upper to lower legs
25 Connections between femur and tibia

26 Connections between femur and tibia. Azimene
27 Deep nerves. Azimene
28 Right genicular arteries. Azimene
29 Left genicular arteries. Azimene
30 Adductor muscle (?)

Aquarius

1 Right tibial nerve (Obesity)
2 Left tibial nerve
3 Right fibula
4 Left fibula
5 Nerve of right fibula
6 Nerve of left fibula (Sight)
7 Right saphenous veins
8 Left saphenous veins (Anaemia)
9 Skin of right lower leg
10 Skin of left lower leg
11 Right cruciate ligaments
12 Left cruciate ligaments
13 Right tibial artery (Rheumatic fever)
14 Left tibial artery
15 Lymph vessels of right lower leg
16 Lymph vessels of left lower leg
17 Spinal nervous system
18 Spinal nervous system. Azimene. (Chronic glomerulonephritis)
19 Spinal nervous system. Azimene. (Spine)
20 Spinal nervous system
21 Spinal nervous system
22 Right gastrocnemius muscle? (Appendicitis)
23 Left gastrocnemius muscle? (Rheumatism)
24 Right tibialis anterior muscle?
25 Left tibialis anterior muscle? (Alcoholism, abscess)
26 Right fibula (Nervous debility)
27 Left fibula (Goitre)
28 Right tibia

29 Left tibia (Neuritis)
30 Connections – between what is not clear

Pisces

1 Right calcaneum
2 Left calcaneum
3 Nerves of right foot (Appendix)
4 Nerves of left foot (Asthma)
5 Right cuboid bone
6 Left cuboid bone
7 Right talus
8 Left talus
9 Right metatarsals (Rheumatic fever)
10 Left metatarsals (Enteric fever)
11 Lymph vessels of foot
12 Plantar artery of right foot
13 Plantar artery of left foot
14 Right cutaneous veins
15 Left cutaneous veins
16 Cruciate? ligaments of right foot
17 Cruciate? ligaments of left foot
18 Extensor muscles of right toes
19 Extensor muscles of left toes
20 Right fibula muscle?
21 Left fibula muscle? (Enteric fever)
22 Achilles tendon of right foot (Insanity, appendicitis)
23 Achilles tendon of left foot (Spine)
24 Right distal tibio-fibular joint?
25 Left distal tibio-fibular joint? (Cancer, gout)
26 Plantar nerves (Suicide)
27 Phalanges of right foot (Chronic glomerulonephritis)
28 Phalanges of left foot (Tuberculosis)
29 Toenails of right foot
30 Toenails of left foot

Maurice Wemyss gives a slightly different assessment of the degree areas. Wemyss was an Edinburgh lawyer with highly original ideas on the sign rulerships. Two volumes of his five-part scholarly work, *The Wheel of Life or Scientific Astrology*, are devoted to medical astrology and are crammed full of interesting data and case histories. He wrote two other medical volumes before his death. Apparently his publisher, who was also an astrologer, was alarmed by the transits around that time and made a hasty journey north. Alas, too late! The manuscripts had already been consigned to the flames with great satisfaction by the Presbyterian sister who had kept house for Wemyss.

Aries/Libra

Degrees	Anatomical	Pathological
0	Skull	Amputation
1	Skull	
2	Skull	Asthma, cramp
3	Skull	
4	Forehead	Muscle strain, accidents
5	Forehead	Cuts
6	Forehead	Bruising, scratching, bites
7	Teeth	Adenoids
8	Nose	Bruising, burns
9	Nose	Burns and blisters
10	Nose	High fever, burns
11	Nose	Diphtheria
12	Nose	
13	Eyes	Food poisoning, alcoholism
14	Eyes	Cataract, excess eating
15	Under eye area	
16	Under eye area	
17	Cheeks, ears	Suicide, asthma
18	Cheeks, ears	
19	Bladder	Bladder problems
20	Bladder	
21	Bladder	
22	Bladder	Tuberculosis
23	Bladder	Tuberculosis
24	Bladder	
25	Mouth	
26	Mouth	Carbuncles

27	Chin	Abscesses
28	Chin	
29	Beginning of neck	Stroke

Taurus/Scorpio

0	Top of neck	
1	Top of neck	
2	Top of neck	
3	Top of neck	Epilepsy
4	Sense of touch	Contagious diseases
5	Sense of touch	
6	Sense of touch	
7	Sense of touch	Adenoids
8	Eyeball	Alcoholism, deafness
9	Mucous membrane, eyes	Catarrh and colds
10	Mucous membrane, eyes	
11	Mucous membrane, eyes	Asthma
12	Adam's apple area	Sydenham's chorea, convulsions
13	Adam's apple area	
14	Circulatory system	Growths
15	Bottom of neck	Diphtheria
16	Shoulders begin	Colour blindness, cramp
17	Shoulders begin	Appendicitis
18	Shoulders begin	Tumours
19	Shoulders begin	
20	Bronchial tubes	Bronchitis
21	Bronchial tubes	Abnormal births
22	Bronchial tubes	Crushing injuries
23	Bronchial tubes	
24	Bronchial tubes	Dislocations
25	Collarbone	Fracture
26	Collarbone	
27	Collarbone	
28	Collarbone	Rheumatic fever, alcoholism
29	End of shoulders	
30	Beginning of arms	

Gemini/Sagittarius

0	U		
1	P		
2	P	Upper lung	
3	E	Optic nerve	Eye defects, colour blindness
4	R	Eyes	Blindness
5		Eyes	

6	A	Eyes	
7	R	Eyes	Adenoids
8	M	Elbows	Meningitis, tuberculosis
9		Elbows	Deafness
10	L	Elbows	
11	O	Elbows	Bites
12	W	Elbows	Accidents involving travelling
13	E	Elbows	
14	R	Elbows	Travel sickness
15		Elbows	Diphtheria
16	A	Breathing system	Breathing problems
17	R	Breathing system	
18	M	Breathing system	Mutism, blisters, burns
19		Speech	Blisters and burns
20	T	Wrists	
21	H	Wrists	
22	E	Wrists	
23		Lower lungs	
24	A	Lower lungs	
25	R	Lower lungs	
26	M	Lower lungs	
27	S	Lower lungs	
28		Lower lungs	Whooping cough
29		Fingers	
30		Fingers	

Cancer/Capricorn

0	Top of trunk	Chills and colds
1	Top of trunk	Indigestion, catarrh, flu
2	Top of trunk	Chronic rheumatic complaints
3	Top of trunk	
4	Ears	Deafness
5	Ears	Adenoids, stroke
6	Ears	
7	Kidneys	Adenoids
8	Bones	Broken bones, arthritis
9	Heart	Heart disease
10	Heart	Cardiac oedema
11	Heart	
12	Heart	
13	Heart	
14	Heart	Cataract
15	Heart	
16	Heart	
17	Heart	
18	Heart	Tumours
19	Gall-bladder	Constipation, gall-stones, mutism
20	Gall-bladder	Drowning, choking, suffocation

21		Gall-bladder	
22		Gall-bladder	
23		Gall-bladder	
24		Gall-bladder	
25		Gall-bladder	Breathing problems
26		Gall-bladder	
27		Gall-bladder	
28		Gall-bladder	Crushing injuries
29		Gall-bladder	
30		Bottom of trunk	

Leo/Aquarius

0		Top of lumbar region	
1		Top of lumbar region	
2		Top of lumbar region	
3		Top of lumbar region	Biliousness
4		Sense of smell	
5		Sense of smell	
6		Sense of smell	
7		Kidneys	Oedema
8		Skin	Eczema
9		Skin	
10		Skin	
11		Skin	
12		Skin	
13		Skin	
14		Skin	Abscesses
15		Skin	
16		Skin	
17		Skin	Appendicitis, asthma
18		Skin	
19		Skin	Bladder problems
20	O	Skin	Diarrhoea
21	V	Skin	Strokes, tuberculosis
22	E	Bladder	
23	R	Bladder	
24		Bladder	
25	W	Bladder	Burns, inflammation
26	E	Bladder	Obesity, carbuncles
27	I	Bladder	Poisoning, food poisoning
28	G	Bladder	Alcoholism
29	H	Bladder	
30	T	Bottom of lumbar region	

Virgo/Pisces

0	U	Duodenum	
1	P	Duodenum	
2	P	Duodenum	Suicide

.3	E		Duodenum	
4	R		Duodenum	Cuts
5			Duodenum	
6	B		Duodenum	
7	O		Duodenum	
8	W		Duodenum	Dysentery
9	E		Duodenum	Dysentery
10	L	D	Duodenum	Dysentery
11		R	Duodenum	
12		O	Duodenum	
13		W	Duodenum	Alcoholism
14		N	Duodenum	
15		I	Duodenum	
16		N	Duodenum	
17		G	Duodenum	
18			Duodenum	
19	L		Duodenum	Constipation
20	O		Duodenum	Diarrhoea
21	W		Duodenum	
22	E		Appendix	Appendicitis
23	R		Appendix	Appendicitis
24			Appendix	
25	B		Appendix	
26	O		Appendix	
27	W		Appendix	
28	E		Appendix	
29	L		Appendix	
30			Appendix	

Once the chart has been assessed for diseases to which its owner is liable, it is, according to Wemyss, possible to work out by means of a table which he devised, at which age these afflictions are most likely to occur. For example, heart disease is said to be associated with 10 degrees Cancer and/or Capricorn. From the table below it can be seen that the sixty-ninth year is the most risky for those with these degrees badly aspected. However, simply because a person has a particular degree afflicted does not necessarily mean that illness is inevitable in the year corresponding to it. There would also have to be strong indications from other natal aspects, as well as transits and progressions, to increase the likelihood of its happening.

Table 3. Age – sign correlation

Years of age	Degrees of sign Aries/Libra	Years of age	Degrees of sign Taurus/Scorpio	Years of age	Degrees of sign Gemini/Saggitarius
36	0 – 2½	24	0 – 2½	12	0 – 2½
35	2½ – 5	23	2½ – 5	11	2½ – 5
34	5 – 7½	22	5 – 7½	10	5 – 7½
33	7½ – 10	21	7½ – 10	9	7½ – 10
32	10 – 12½	20	10 – 12½	8	10 – 12½
31	12½ – 15	19	12½ – 15	7	12½ – 15
30	15 – 17½	18	15 – 17½	6	15 – 17½
29	17½ – 20	17	17½ – 20	5	17½ – 20
28	20 – 22½	16	20 – 22½	4	20 – 22½
27	22½ – 25	15	22½ – 25	3	22½ – 25
26	25 – 27½	14	25 – 27½	2	25 – 27½
25	27½ – 30	13	27½ – 30	1	27½ – 30

Years of age	Degrees of sign Cancer/Capricorn	Years of age	Degrees of sign Leo/Aquarius	Years of age	Degrees of sign Virgo/Pisces
72	0 – 2½	60	0 – 2½	48	0 – 2½
71	2½ – 5	59	2½ – 5	47	2½ – 5
70	5 – 7½	58	5 – 7½	46	5 – 7½
69	7½ – 10	57	7½ – 10	45	7½ – 10
68	10 – 12½	56	10 – 12½	44	10 – 12½
67	12½ – 15	55	12½ – 15	43	12½ – 15
66	15 – 17½	54	15 – 17½	42	15 – 17½
65	17½ – 20	53	17½ – 20	41	17½ – 20
64	20 – 22½	52	20 – 22½	40	20 – 22½
63	22½ – 25	51	22½ – 25	39	22½ – 25
62	25 – 27½	50	25 – 27½	38	25 – 27½
61	27½ – 30	49	27½ – 30	37	27½ – 30

The fixed stars have long been considered to be significant in medical astrology. They were extensively used in decumbiture. The medieval interpretations were somewhat melodramatic to say the least, so only the planetary natures of the most important stars are given below. De Vore's *Encyclopaedia of Astrology* contains a more complete list of fixed stars.

Because of the precession of the equinoxes, the fixed stars gain approximately one degree of longitude every seventy years, which is about fifty seconds a year. The positions listed in Table 4 are the approximate positions for 1990. To find the positions for charts referring to other years, add or subtract fifty seconds for each year from 1990.

The orb allowed for fixed stars is not normally more than one degree, and usually only the conjunction is considered. However, Marcia Starck has carried out some interesting work on eye disorders. She has found that the conjunction, square or opposition of certain fixed stars to the angles, Sun, Moon and other planets is often found in these conditions. Those which seem to be most actively involved are the Pleiades, the Hyades, the Asselli, Antares and Spiculum.

Table 4. Positions of the fixed stars in 1990

Sign	Name of Star	Nature	Approximate 1990 Position
Aries	Vertex	Mars, Moon	27.47
Taurus	Capulus	Mars, Mercury	24.09
	Algol	Saturn, Jupiter	26.07
	Pleiades	Moon, Mars	29.56
Gemini	Hyades	Venus	5.45
	Aldebaran	Mars	9.44
	Rigel	Jupiter, Saturn	16.47
	El Nath	Mars	22.31
	Bellatrix	Mars, Mercury	20.54
	Mintaka	Saturn, Jupiter	22.20
	Ensis	Mars, Moon	22.59
	Betelgeuze	Mars, Mercury	28.42
Cancer	Sirius	Jupiter, Mars	14.03
	Castor	Venus, Saturn	20.12

Table 4. (cont.)

	Pollux	Mars	23.11
	Procyon	Mercury, Mars	25.45
Leo	Praecepe	Mars, Moon	7.11
	N. Assellus	Mars, Sun	7.29
	S. Assellus	Mars, Sun	8.40
	Al Jabbah	Saturn, Mercury	27.51
	Alphard	Saturn, Venus	27.14
	Regulus	Mars	29.47
Virgo	Denebola	Mercury, Venus	21.43
	Copula	Moon, Venus	25.02
	Labrum	Mercury, Venus	26.39
Libra	Seginus	Mercury, Saturn	17.36
	Foramen	Saturn, Jupiter	22.07
	Arcturus	Mars, Jupiter	24.11
	Spica	Venus, Mars	23.47
Scorpio	Princeps	Mercury, Saturn	3.06
	Alphecca	Venus, Mercury	12.14
	S. Chelae	Saturn, Venus	15.02
	N. Chelae	Jupiter, Mars	19.19
	Unukhalai	Saturn, Mars	22.00
Sagittarius	Yed Prior	Mars, Saturn	2.15
	Antares	Mercury, Mars	9.43
	Rastaban	Saturn, Venus	11.54
	Aculeus	Mars, Moon	25.43
	Acumen	Mars, Moon	28.39
Capricorn	Spiculum	Mars, Moon	0.36
	Vega	Venus, Mercury	15.16
	Facies	Sun, Mars	8.16
	Manubrium	Sun, Mars	14.56
Aquarius	Altair	Saturn, Mercury	1.43
	Giedi	Venus, Mars	3.46
	Dagih	Saturn, Venus	4.00
	Oculus	Saturn, Venus	4.40
	Sadalsund	Saturn, Mercury	23.04
Pisces	Fomalhaut	Venus, Mercury	3.48
	Markab	Mars, Mercury	23.26
	Scheat	Mars, Mercury	20.19

ARABIAN PARTS

There are many Arabians parts other than the familiar Part of Fortune. They are points of sensitivity in the chart and are triggered by lunations, full moons, eclipses and transits and progressions. Those relevant to medical astrology are:

The Part of Sickness   – Ascendant plus Mars minus Saturn
The Part of Death   – Ascendant plus the 8th-house cusp minus Moon
The Part of Surgery   – Ascendant plus Saturn minus Mars

According to some experts equal house cusps should always be used in calculating Arabian Parts. To find the appropriate Part, convert the Ascendant and planets concerned into zodiacal longitude using the table below.

o Aries	= 0	o Leo	= 120	o Sagittarius	= 240
o Taurus	= 30	o Virgo	= 150	o Capricorn	= 270
o Gemini	= 60	o Libra	= 180	o Aquarius	= 300
o Cancer	= 90	o Scorpio	= 210	o Pisces	= 330

For example, in a chart where the Ascendant is 26.14 Virgo, Mars is 21.46 Aquarius and Saturn is 1.54 Capricorn, the Part of Sickness is calculated as follows

Ascendant	= 150 + 26.14 = 176.14
+ Mars	= 300 + 21.46 = 321.46
	497.60
− Saturn	= 270 + 1.54 = 271.54
	226.06

The Part of Sickness is 226.06 degrees = 16.06 degrees Scorpio.

REFERENCES

Addey, John, *Harmonics in Astrology*, L. N. Fowler & Co., London 1976
Carter, Charles, *An Encyclopaedia of Psychological Astrology*, The Theosophical Publishing House, London, 1937

Daath, Heinrich, *Medical Astrology*, L. N. Fowler & Co., London, 1914

Ebertin, Elsbeth and Reinhold, *Anatomische Entsprechungen der Tierkreisgrade*, Ebertin Verlag, Aalen, 1971

Harvey, Charles, 'Astrology and Genetics – Haemophilia' in *Astrology and Medicine Newsletter*, No. 3, November 1987

Lilly, William, *Christian Astrology*, 1647. Regulus Facsimile Editions, London 1985

Machon, Gregorio Luis Lozano, *Los 360 grados del zodiaco astrologico*, Minuesa, Madrid, 1985

Millard, Dr Margaret, 'The Brain and the Immune System' in *Astrology and Medicine Newsletter*, No. 3, November 1987

Starck, Marcia, *Key to Holistic Health*, Seek-It Publications, Birmingham, Michigan, 1982

Vore, Nicholas de, *Encyclopaedia of Astrology*, Littlefield, Adams & Co., New York, 1980

Wemyss, Maurice, *The Wheel of Life or Scientific Astrology*, 5 vols., L. N. Fowler & Co., London, 1927–45

5

~∂⌐

THE DECUMBITURE CHART

Although many astrologers of earlier times were profoundly concerned with using their art to shed light on the workings of the soul, the main emphasis tended to be on outer manifestations. Illness and disease are 'events' which take place at the interface between the psyche and the environment. This interface is the body, or more correctly the body-mind complex, so taking a closer look at earlier methods would appear to be a worthwhile and necessary part of any serious study of medical astrology.

The first thing that becomes obvious in so-called 'traditional' astrology is that, although the building blocks – planets, aspects, signs and houses – are much the same as in the more familiar psychological astrology of today, the rules for interpretation at times differ widely because the emphasis is different. It is not easy to make much sense of traditional medical astrology without a basic understanding of traditional rules. Because decumbiture, which is a specialized medical form of horary astrology, is a relatively unknown subject, I will go into the setting up of the chart and its interpretation in some detail. Very few decumbiture practitioners will use all of the information available, but it is useful to have it gathered in one place.

The outer planets, of course, had not been discovered when these rules were drawn up and therefore do not feature in this chapter. They are, however, entered in decumbiture charts nowadays and interpreted according to our present-day understanding of their properties.

The main functions of the decumbiture chart are to show:

1. The nature of the complaint and part of the body affected
2. What caused it
3. The prognosis
4. The practitioner's/astrologer's part in the therapeutic relationship
5. Critical phases in the course of the illness
6. What measures are indicated

The decumbiture (from the Latin *de*, meaning 'down', and *cumbere*, 'to lie'), is, in the strict sense, a chart drawn up for the time a person is so overcome by illness that they must lie down or take to their bed. However, many medical problems are not severe enough to force the patient to bed, so another suitable time usually has to be selected.

TIMING THE CHART

William Lilly, whose *Christian Astrology* was published in 1647, is one of the greatest and most accessible authorities on traditional astrology. His rules for choosing the moment to erect the chart are as follows:

... we ought carefully to take the exact time of the parties first falling sick, *viz.* the houre as neer as can be had, not that moment when first the Patient felt a smatch of it, but that very time when first he was so ill, or so extremely oppressed, that he was enforced to take to his Bed, or to repose.

Secondly, if that cannot be had, then accept of that time when the sick parties *Urine* was first carried to somebody, to enquire of the Disease, whether the party enquired of was a Physitian or not.

Thirdly, if no such thing can be had, let the Physitian take the time of his owne first speaking with, or accesse to the Patient, or when first the *Urine* was brought unto him ...

Decumbiture practitioners tend to use the first moment that the patient has their full attention in the consulting room.

Erecting the Chart

Once the moment has been selected and timed, the chart is drawn up. Traditionally Regiomontanus houses are used, but some astrologers prefer to use one of the other quadrant systems such as Placidus, Koch or Porphyry. Some astrological computer software offers the option of Regiomontanus cusps, and they are also given in *Tools of Astrology* by Maries Lorenz. The co-ordinates used are the latitude and longitude of the place where the consultation occurs.

Radicality

Perhaps because of the difficulties of timing, a screening system is built into horary. Before it can be used the chart must be checked to see if it is radical, in other words fit to be judged. There are three methods of deciding – strictures, planetary hours and aptness.

Strictures on Judgement

A stricture is a feature that gives warning that a chart should not be read. In practice, some medical astrologers use strictures as cautions rather than vetos, but note the results carefully.

1. If the Ascendant is less than 3 degrees, especially in the signs of short ascension (Capricorn to Gemini inclusive), unless the patient is very young, or the body type or blemishes agree with the sign on the Ascendant.

2. If the Ascendant is 27 degrees or more, unless the age of the patient corresponds to the degree of the Ascendant, or the decumbiture is taken for the exact time that the patient took to bed.

3. If the Moon is in the Via Combusta, that is, between 15 degrees Libra and 15 degrees Scorpio, unless the patient's Ascendant falls within this zodiacal area.

4. If the Moon is Void of Course, that is, it does not make an aspect to any other planet before leaving the sign it is in. Some practitioners do use a chart having a Void of Course Moon, but give the judgement that nothing will come of the matter, that it is out of the control of the questioner. Lilly says that it is less unsafe to judge a chart with a Void of Course Moon if the principal significator is strong, or where it is in Taurus, Cancer, Sagittarius or Pisces.

5. If Saturn is in the seventh house, the astrologer's/practitioner's judgement may be faulty.

6. If the seventh-house cusp is afflicted, or if its ruler is retrograde and badly placed. Again this points to faulty judgement on the part of the practitioner.

7. If Saturn is conjunct the Ascendant or in the first house, especially where it is retrograde, or if the ruler of the Ascendant is combust, that is, within eight degrees of the Sun. These are normally regarded as strictures, although it can be argued that, in medical cases, it is still possible to use such a chart.

Aptness

For some astrologers, the acid test of radicality is whether the chart really does seem to describe the situation in question. If the Ascendant, the planets in the first house and the ruler of the Ascendant do describe the patient, and the sixth-house cusp, its ruler and any planets placed there describe the patient's complaint, then the chart is valid.

Planetary Hours

The most important traditional method of testing validity is to check whether the ruler of the hour for which the chart was erected is of the same nature as the Ascendant or the ruler of the Ascendant (see Figure 4). The concept of each hour of the day being ruled by a particular planet is an ancient one. Each day of the week is associated with one particular planet as follows:

> The Sun rules Sunday.
> The Moon rules Monday.
> Mars rules Tuesday (Mardi in French).
> Mercury rules Wednesday (Mercredi in French).
> Jupiter rules Thursday (after Thor, the Norse god who is similar to Jupiter in many ways).

Venus rules Friday (Vendredi in French. Freya is the Norse equivalent of Venus).

Saturn rules Saturday.

In the system of planetary hours, the first hour of any day is ruled by the planet which rules the day. The subsequent hours are ruled in sequence by the planets in increasing order of speed, or decreasing order of length of cycle. In other words, the order is Saturn, Jupiter, Mars, Sun, Venus, Mercury and Moon. Once the Moon is reached, the whole process starts again with Saturn.

The elegance of the system becomes apparent on setting out the planetary hours for the week. It can be seen that each day automatically starts with its own ruler, as shown in Table 5.

If the first hour of each day was taken as starting at midnight and each planetary hour consisted of sixty minutes, life would be simple. Alas, that is not the case. The day starts at sunrise, and although some ancient authors are believed to have divided the day into sixty-minute hours, the more common system is more complicated. The times for sunrise and sunset must be known, then the hours between sunrise and sunset are divided into twelve equal parts. These are the first twelve planetary hours. The hours from sunset to the next sunrise are then divided likewise to make up the twelve planetary hours of the night.

The first reaction on coming across this complicated procedure is to want to dismiss the whole thing as being just too much of a nuisance. This is certainly what Zadkiel did when he published his bowdlerized version of Lilly's *Christian Astrology*. However, the planetary hours are more than a means of checking whether or not a chart is valid. They are a fundamental component in choosing the time to harvest and prepare herbs, to give medicines, and to perform any surgical procedures. So it seems that a little effort will yield much of advantage.

I am greatly indebted to the French astrologer, Denis Labouré, for showing me the following simple method for calculating the planetary hours, using Placidus house cusps. As the Placidus house system is purely time-based, each of the houses represents two planetary hours. The first hour starts at dawn with the Ascendant. Moving clockwise, the area between the Ascendant and the twelfth-house cusp represents the first two planetary hours, that between the twelfth and the eleventh

Planetary hour rulers

	DAWN 1	2	3	4	5	6	7	8	9	10	11	12	SUNSET 1	2	3	4	5	6	7	8	9	10	11	12
SUNDAY	☉	♀	☿	☽	♄	♃	♂	☉	♀	☿	☽	♄	♃	♂	☉	♀	☿	☽	♄	♃	♂	☉	♀	☿
MONDAY	☽	♄	♃	♂	☉	♀	☿	☽	♄	♃	♂	☉	♀	☿	☽	♄	♃	♂	☉	♀	☿	☽	♄	♃
TUESDAY	♂	☉	♀	☿	☽	♄	♃	♂	☉	♀	☿	☽	♄	♃	♂	☉	♀	☿	☽	♄	♃	♂	☉	♀
WEDNESDAY	☿	☽	♄	♃	♂	☉	♀	☿	☽	♄	♃	♂	☉	♀	☿	☽	♄	♃	♂	☉	♀	☿	☽	♄
THURSDAY	♃	♂	☉	♀	☿	☽	♄	♃	♂	☉	♀	☿	☽	♄	♃	♂	☉	♀	☿	☽	♄	♃	♂	☉
FRIDAY	♀	☿	☽	♄	♃	♂	☉	♀	☿	☽	♄	♃	♂	☉	♀	☿	☽	♄	♃	♂	☉	♀	☿	☽
SATURDAY	♄	♃	♂	☉	♀	☿	☽	♄	♃	♂	☉	♀	☿	☽	♄	♃	♂	☉	♀	☿	☽	♄	♃	♂

the third and fourth hours, and so on. The Midheaven represents the end of the sixth daytime planetary hour, while the Descendant corresponds to sunset. The sixth house is made up of the first two nocturnal planetary hours, and so it continues on round to the Ascendant.

The division between the two planetary hours in any house is found by dividing the house exactly in two. To find the planetary hour of the decumbiture, or indeed any chart, find the house in which the Sun falls, using Placidus house cusps. Figure 2 illustrates this. Here the Sun is in the eighth house. It is therefore in either the ninth or tenth daytime planetary hour. Since it is clearly in the second part of the house, reckoned clockwise from the Ascendant, the Sun is in the tenth planetary hour. If this represented a chart drawn up on a Monday, one can see by looking along the line for Monday in the table of planetary hour rulers (Table 5) that the ruler of the tenth daytime hour is Jupiter. If, instead, this was a Thursday chart, the ruler would be the Sun.

Computer owners may be pleased to hear that the Electric Almanac, a free promotional program from Matrix Software, contains a useful planetary-hours option.

Using this system, a chart is not valid unless the ruler of the hour is in some way in harmony with the Ascendant or the lord (ruler) of the Ascendant. There are several ways that this can be satisfied:

1. If the ruler of the Ascendant and the ruler of the hour are the same, as, for example, where Virgo or Gemini is rising and Mercury is the ruler of the hour.

2. If the ruler of the hour is of the same triplicity as the Ascendant. The rulers of the triplicities are given in Ptolemy's table (Table 7, p. 122). An example of this would be where Jupiter is the ruler of a chart that is drawn up after sunset and the Ascendant is in a fire sign. Jupiter is the nocturnal ruler of the fiery triplicity.

3. If the ruler of the hour and the Ascendant are of the same nature. Each of the signs and planets has two qualities; they are either hot or cold, and either moist or dry. The fire and air signs are hot, while the negative signs, earth and water, are cold. The fire signs, as expected, are classed as dry, as are the earth signs. Air and water are moist. For

example, if Venus is the ruler and Cancer ascends, the chart is valid because they are both of the same nature. The qualities are given in Table 6.

4. If the ruler of the hour is in strong aspect to the Ascendant, or its ruler, or to the lord of the triplicity of the Ascendant. For example, if 10 degrees Gemini is rising in a daytime chart, the chart is valid if the ruler of the hour makes a close major aspect to 10 degrees Gemini, or to Mercury, the ruler of the Ascendant, or to Saturn, the daytime ruler of the air signs.

Table 6. Qualities of signs and planets

Signs			
Aries	hot and dry	**Taurus**	cold and dry
Gemini	hot and moist	**Cancer**	cold and moist
Leo	hot and dry	**Virgo**	cold and dry
Libra	hot and moist	**Scorpio**	cold and moist
Sagittarius	hot and dry	**Capricorn**	cold and dry
Aquarius	hot and moist	**Pisces**	cold and moist
Planets			
Sun	hot and dry	**Moon**	cold and moist
Mercury	cold and dry	**Venus**	cold and moist
Mars	hot and dry	**Jupiter**	hot and moist
Saturn	cold and dry		

Figure 3 (see page 133) shows a decumbiture chart drawn up at the first visit of a patient we shall call Tom. The chart is radical on all counts. There are no strictures, and the Moon, ruler of the hour, makes a close sextile aspect with Venus, daytime ruler of the triplicity of the Ascendant. The chief significator of Tom is Mercury, which is in its own sign in the ninth house, representing, among other things, foreign countries and higher learning. Tom is an academic who has recently returned from abroad, where he thinks his present complaint originated. The decumbiture Ascendant is also conjunct Tom's natal Ascendant, so the chart clearly indicates the situation in hand.

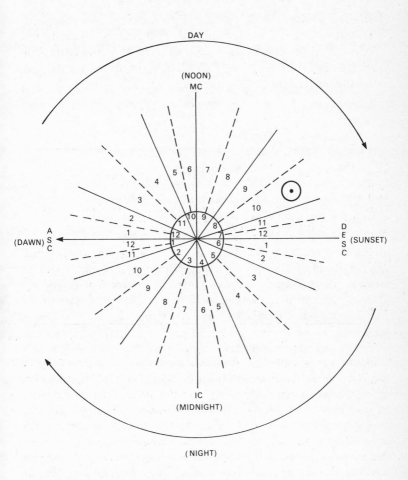

Figure 2 Calculating the planetary hour

Before starting to prepare the chart, it is useful to gather together all the materials required. This may sound too elementary to mention, but the observation comes from the heart after many wasted and frustrating hours. It is probably easiest to copy out the tables and keep them together in loose-leaf form. You will need:

1. A chart form which allows space for the details of all the features you intend to use. The one I have devised is shown in Figure 3 (see page 133).
2. A list of fixed stars (see Table 4, page 107).
3. A table of rulers of planetary hours (Table 5, page 116).
4. A table of qualities (see Table 6, page 118).
5. Ptolemy's table of essential dignities (see Table 7, page 122).
6. Lilly's table of dignities and debilities (see Table 8, page 126).
7. A list of average motions of the planets (see page 125).
8. A list of antiscions (see Table 10, page 128).

The chart is filled in the usual way, but the aspect lines are omitted. Instead, the planets, including Uranus, Neptune and Pluto, are entered beneath the appropriate number in the area marked 'Degrees and Planets'. This method, developed by Olivia Barclay, is particularly useful as the linear form allows past and future aspects to be seen at a glance.

After entering the planetary positions, we need to consider their dignities and debilities and to fill in the appropriate grid on the chart form. It is useful to circle any planets that are in their own dignity or in mutual reception (see Table 7).

Planetary Strengths

Modern astrology scarcely takes note of the strengths of the planets, but traditionally they were of primary importance. A planet is said to be strong when it has essential dignity by being either in its own sign, exaltation, triplicity, term or face, or is in mutual reception with another planet by sign, exaltation, triplicity, term or face. It is debilitated or weak when it is in its detriment or fall, or when it has no essential dignities. It is then said to be peregrine.

Looking at Ptolemy's table, we see that the signs are in the first column. Information about the planets in a particular sign may be gained by reading along the rows.

The second column lists the planet or planets ruling the sign on the left. The Sun and Moon are both followed by the letters D and N, the other planets by only one or other letter. D means diurnal, signifying that the sign concerned is the daytime house of that planet. N stands for nocturnal and shows that the planet has its night-time house in that sign. Leo is both the day and night house of the Sun, while, similarly, the Moon has the complete tenancy of Cancer.

Dignity by Sign

A planet is said to be in its own sign when it is in the sign it rules. For example, Jupiter is in its own sign in Sagittarius and Pisces, the Sun in Leo, and Mercury in Virgo and Gemini.

Exaltation

The exaltations appear in column three. The figure after the symbol refers to the exact degree of the sign on the left in which the planet is especially favoured.

Ptolemy has an interesting explanation of the exaltations, but one which assumes that the centre of the world is in the northern hemisphere. The Sun is exalted in Aries, because it is in this sign when it crosses from the lower to the upper hemisphere and its heat increases. It is in its fall in Libra for the same reason – the heat is now decreasing.

As Saturn opposes the Sun by quality as well as by natural house position, it is therefore exalted in Libra and in its fall in Aries. The Moon, the night ruler of the earth signs, starts to increase its light in the first earth sign, Taurus, where it is therefore exalted, and is in its fall in Scorpio.

Jupiter, which is associated with the north, is in its exaltation in Cancer, which is where the Sun reaches its most northerly point. Its fall is consequently in the polar opposite sign, Capricorn. Mars, whose nature is fiery, is even more so in Capricorn, which is furthest south,

SIGNS			EXALTATION		TRIPLICITY		TERMS										FACES						DETRIMENT	FALL
					DAY	NIGHT																		
♈	♂	D	☉	19	☉	♃	♃	6	♀	14	☿	21	♂	26	♄	30	♂	10	☉	20	♀	30	♀	♄
♉	♀	N	☽	3	♀	☽	♀	8	☿	15	♃	22	♄	26	♂	30	☿	10	☽	20	♄	30	♂	
♊	☿	D	☊	3	♄	☿	☿	7	♃	14	♀	21	♄	25	♂	30	♃	10	♂	20	☉	30	♃	
♋	☽	DN	♃	15	♂	♂	♂	6	♃	13	☿	20	♀	27	♄	30	♀	10	☿	20	☽	30	♄	♂
♌	☉	DN			☉	♃	♄	6	☿	13	♀	19	♃	25	♂	30	♄	10	♃	20	♂	30	♄	
♍	☿	N	☿	15	♀	☽	☿	7	♀	13	♃	18	♄	24	♂	30	☉	10	♀	20	☿	30	♃	♀
♎	♀	D	♄	21	♄	☿	♄	6	♀	11	♃	19	♀	24	♂	30	☽	10	♄	20	♃	30	♂	☉
♏	♂	N			♂	♂	♂	6	♃	14	♀	21	☿	27	♄	30	♂	10	☉	20	♀	30	♀	☽
♐	♃	D	☋	3	☉	♃	♃	8	♀	14	☿	19	♄	25	♂	30	☿	10	☽	20	♄	30	☿	
♑	♄	N	♂	28	♀	☽	♀	6	☿	12	♃	19	♂	25	♄	30	♃	10	♂	20	☉	30	☽	♃
♒	♄	D			♄	☿	♄	6	☿	12	♀	20	♃	25	♂	30	♀	10	☿	20	☽	30	☉	
♓	♃	N	♀	27	♂	♂	♀	8	♃	14	☿	20	♂	26	♄	30	♄	10	♃	20	♂	30	☿	☿

Table 7. Ptolemy's table of the essential dignities and debilities of the planets

and is thus exalted there, and in its fall in Cancer, sign of the north. Venus, being of a moist nature, becomes even more so with the dampness of spring; thus it is exalted in Pisces and in its fall in Virgo. Mercury, on the other hand, is dry and is naturally exalted in Virgo, which signifies the start of the dryness of autumn.

Dignity by Triplicity

Column four deals with the triplicities. The twelve signs are divided into the four triplicities still used in modern astrology, but traditionally one planet rules the triplicity for a chart drawn up in the daytime, and another for a chart drawn up at night.

The fiery triplicity, Aries, Leo and Sagittarius, is ruled by the Sun by day and Jupiter by night.

Gemini, Libra and Aquarius, the airy signs, are ruled by Saturn by day and Mercury by night.

In the earthy triplicity, Taurus, Virgo and Capricorn, Venus has domination by day and the Moon by night.

By way of contrast, the watery signs, Cancer, Scorpio and Pisces, have only one ruler, whether by day or night, and that is Mars.

Dignity by Term

The terms come next. Looking along the top line of the table, we read Jupiter 6, Venus 14, Mercury 21, Mars 26 and Saturn 30. This means that any planet which is found between 0 degrees Aries and 5 degrees 59 minutes Aries is in the terms of Jupiter. If Jupiter is here, it is said to be in its own terms. Venus's terms run from 6 degrees to 13 degrees 59 minutes Aries, Mercury's from 14 degrees to 20 degrees 59 minutes, and so on. The Sun and Moon have no terms.

Dignity by Face

Each sign is divided into three decanates or sectors of ten degrees. In each decanate one particular planet is said to be in its own face. It is interesting to look down the first column of the faces and note that the planets follow the order of the days of the week they rule. For example, the first column of faces starts with Mars, the ruler of Aries which rules Tuesday; below it is Mercury, ruler of Wednesday, followed by Jupiter (Thursday), Venus (Friday), Saturn (Saturday) and so on. The list is continuous. It always follows the same order right down the first list of faces, and takes up where it left off at the top of the next column.

Even more interesting is to follow the sequence of planets reading along the rows. Again there is a logical pattern, this time following the length of the planetary cycles. Mars starts off once again as the ruler of Aries, followed by the planets in decreasing order of length of cycle – Sun, Venus, Mercury, Moon. The sequence starts again with the heaviest and slowest planet, Saturn, then Jupiter, and so on.

Looking along the top line of the table, under the faces of Aries, a planet which is placed between o degrees Aries and 9 degrees 59 minutes Aries is in Mars's face. From 10 degrees to 19 degrees 59 minutes it will be in the Sun's face; and from 20 degrees up to the end of the sign in the face of Venus.

Planets in their Detriment

The last two columns deal with the debilities of planets. Planets are in their detriment in the signs which are opposite those they rule. For example, the Moon is in its detriment in Capricorn, and Saturn in its detriment in both Cancer and Leo.

Planets in their Fall

Planets are in their fall in the sign opposite the one in which they are exalted.

Mutual Reception

We are used to the concept of mutual reception by sign, where, for example, Mars is in Cancer and the Moon is in Aries. Each planet is in the sign of the other's rulership. Traditionally it is also possible for planets to be in mutual reception by exaltation, triplicity, term or face. It is very easy to find if any planets are in mutual reception using the grid form shown. For example, in the decumbiture chart (see Figure 3), Venus is in Saturn's triplicity. To check whether Venus and Saturn are in mutual reception, look along the line to see in which triplicity Saturn falls. It is in Venus's, therefore Venus and Saturn are in mutual reception.

If a planet is not in essential dignity or in mutual reception, it is said to be peregrine and therefore weak or debilitated. This can be indicated by a star, as shown. Any planets debilitated by being in their detriment or fall can also be highlighted in the same way.

Lilly gives a relative weighting to the dignities and debilities of the planets (see Table 8). There is no mention of mutual reception by triplicity, term or face, but as these are mentioned elsewhere as being valid, it seems safe to assume that they would follow the pattern of sign and exaltation and be given the same value as the corresponding dignity.

House Strengths

Lilly states that the angular houses – the first, fourth, seventh and tenth – are the most powerful. The succedents – the second, fifth, eighth and eleventh – come next in strength, followed by the cadents – the third, sixth, ninth and twelfth. However, he then goes on to give, rather oddly, the relative order of houses as follows:

1, 10, 7, 4, 11, 5, 9, 3, 2, 8, 6, 12

That is, the first house is the most powerful, the tenth house the second, and so on.

Average Motion

The average daily motions of the planets are given below.

Moon –	13 degrees	10 minutes	35 seconds
Sun –	0 degrees	59 minutes	08 seconds
Mercury –	4 degrees	06 minutes	00 seconds
Venus –	1 degree	36 minutes	00 seconds

Table 8. Lilly's table of dignities and debilities

Essential dignities		Debilities	
A planet in its own house or in mutual reception with another planet by house	5	In its detriment	−5
		In its fall	−4
		Peregrine	−5
In its exaltation, or reception by exaltation	4		
In its own triplicity	3		
In its own term	2		
In its own face	1		

Accidental dignities		Accidental debilities	
In the Midheaven or Ascendant	5	In the 12th house	−5
In 7th, 4th or 11th house	4	In the 8th and 6th houses	−2
In 2nd and 5th house	3	Retrograde	−5
In 9th house	2	Slow in motion	−2
In 3rd house	1	♄ ♃ ♂ occidental	−2
Direct	4	♀ ☿ oriental	−2
Fast in motion	2	☽ decreasing in light	−2
♄ ♃ ♂ when oriental	2	Combust of the ☉	−5
☿ and ♀ when occidental	2	Under the ☉ beams	−4
☽ increasing, or occidental	2	Partill ☌ with ♄ or ♂	−5
Free from combustion and ☉ beams	5	Partill ☌ with ☋	−4
Cazimi	5	Besieged of ♄ and ♂	−5
In partill ☌ with ♃ and ♀	5	Partill ☍ of ♄ or ♂	−4
Partill ☌ with ☊	4	Partill □ of ♄ or ♂	−3
In partill △ to ♃ and ♀	4	☌ within 5 degrees of	−5
In partill ✶ to ♃ and ♀	3	Algol	
☌ Regulus	6		
☌ Spica	5		

Mars –	0 degrees	31 minutes	00 seconds
Jupiter –	0 degrees	04 minutes	59 seconds
Saturn –	0 degrees	02 minutes	01 second
Uranus –	0 degrees	00 minutes	42 seconds
Neptune –	0 degrees	00 minutes	24 seconds
Pluto –	0 degrees	00 minutes	14 seconds

Oriental and Occidental

The terms oriental and occidental refer to the position of the planets in relation to the Sun. The superior planets – Saturn, Jupiter and Mars – are oriental of the Sun from the time of making a conjunction to the Sun up to the opposition. They are occidental from the opposition to the time of the next conjunction.

The inferior planets, Mercury and Venus, since they cannot be more than 28 degrees and 48 degrees respectively from the Sun, obviously cannot come to an opposition with the Sun. They are oriental of the Sun when they occupy a lower degree of the sign in which the Sun is placed, or are in the preceding sign. They are occidental when they occupy a greater degree of the Sun sign or are in the following sign. The Moon is occidental of the Sun and increasing in fullness from the time of the conjunction of the new moon up until the opposition or full moon. It is oriental from the full moon, through the third and fourth quarters, to the next new moon.

Combust, Cazimi and Under the Sun's Beams

Planets that are in the same sign as the Sun and are within $8\frac{1}{2}$ degrees of orb are said to be combust and weakened by the power of the Sun. They are more afflicted if the Sun is applying to the conjunction than if it is separating. From $8\frac{1}{2}$ degrees up to 17 degrees apart from the Sun's position, the planet is said to be Under the Sun's Beams and also weakened, though not so much as if it were combust. On the other hand, a planet at the heart of the Sun – within 17 minutes – is said to be cazimi and is greatly increased in strength.

Besieged

A planet is besieged by Mars and Saturn when it lies in the shortest arc between them. This is a Bad Thing! An example of this would be where Mars was at 15 degrees Leo and Saturn was at 10 degrees Virgo. If Venus was positioned anywhere between these two degrees, say at 26 degrees Leo, it would be besieged by Mars and Saturn.

Relative Strengths

Filling in the last line of the grid showing dignities and debilities reveals the relative strengths of the planets.

Fixed Stars

Note if any of the planets or angles conjunct fixed stars. The list of the most commonly used fixed stars and their qualities is found in Table 4 (see page 107). The orb allowed is one degree.

Antiscions

Antiscion points are often used in horary work. They are judged in much the same way as conjunctions, and the effect depends on the nature of the planets involved. For example, the antiscion of Saturn

Planetary position	Antiscion point
Aries	Virgo
Taurus	Leo
Gemini	Cancer
Cancer	Gemini
Leo	Taurus
Virgo	Aries
Libra	Pisces
Scorpio	Aquarius
Sagittarius	Capricorn
Capricorn	Sagittarius
Aquarius	Scorpio
Pisces	Libra

falling on or aspecting another planet generally creates difficulties, while one from Jupiter or Venus may be helpful. One degree orbs are allowed.

To find the antiscion point of a particular planet, you take the point equidistant from that planet and o degrees Cancer and o degrees Capricorn, whichever is the nearer. If that is, say, 19 degrees Virgo, subtract 19 from 30, which equals 11. Looking at the table, we see that Virgo equals Aries. Therefore the antiscion point is 11 degrees Aries. The contrascion point would be 11 degrees Libra.

Midpoints

Midpoints were not used in traditional work, but it can be highly significant when sensitive midpoints are triggered, especially by the heavy planets. A good guide to the interpretation of midpoints is Reinhold Ebertin's book, *The Combination of Stellar Influences*. Some of the more important midpoints relating to health are discussed here in Chapter 3.

Moon's Aspects

The Moon is often the most useful indicator of what is going to happen, as it has the greatest speed of all the heavenly bodies. In traditional astrology a strong distinction is made between separating and applying aspects. Aspects which are separating, that is, more than 6 minutes past exactitude, refer to events which have already taken place. They deal with the past. Applying aspects refer to the future. The last aspect that the Moon makes before leaving the sign it occupies may have an important bearing on, and even be decisive in, the outcome of the matter.

Orbs

The orbs generally used differ slightly from those of today. Planets are said to be in aspect when they are within the sum of the moieties, or half sums of their orbs. Saturn has a moiety of 5 degrees and Venus one of $3\frac{1}{2}$ degrees, making a total of $8\frac{1}{2}$ degrees. So they are within orb up o $8\frac{1}{2}$ degrees of exact aspect. Mercury, Venus and Mars, which each have moieties of $3\frac{1}{2}$ degrees, would be within orb 7 degrees either side of an exact aspect to each other.

Some decumbiture practitioners use standard orbs.

	Orbs	Moieties
Sun	15	8
Moon	12	6
Mercury	7	$3\frac{1}{2}$
Venus	7	$3\frac{1}{2}$
Mars	7	$3\frac{1}{2}$
Jupiter	9	$4\frac{1}{2}$
Saturn	9	$4\frac{1}{2}$

Aspects

Only the major aspects are used, that is, the conjunction, opposition, square, trine and sextile. Aspects which are exact are said to be 'in partill'.

The lighter planets make aspects to the heavier planets. An aspect made in the direction of the natural order of the signs, that is, Aries, Taurus, Gemini, Cancer, etc., is said to be sinister, while one made in the opposite direction, against the natural order, that is, Aries, Pisces, Aquarius, etc., is dexter. For example, Venus in Taurus makes a sinister aspect to Mars in Leo, but a dexter aspect to Saturn in Aquarius. A dexter aspect is stronger than a sinister.

JUDGING THE CHART

The chart is now ready to judge. Note the word is judge and not read, as this type of astrology is very much concerned with weighing up the various factors to see which is strongest and therefore likely to have most influence.

The Significators

The first task is to find the main significators – the planets, houses and house cusps – which represent the problem.

The Ascendant and the ruler of the Ascendant are significators of the patient, with the Moon as co-significator.

The illness is represented by the sign on the sixth-house cusp, its ruler and any planets in the sixth house. Information about the illness can also be gained from the house position and sign of the Moon.

The end of the illness is seen from the fourth house, and the duration can be estimated by the nature of the sign on the cusp. Cardinal signs show that it will end quickly, one way or another. Fixed signs prolong the condition, while the mutables signify that the disease will be variable in nature as well as in its final resolution. The eighth is the house of death and surgery. The seventh represents the astrologer or practitioner. The tenth-house cusp, its ruler and the planets within the tenth house refer to the medicine.

The twelfth house represents hospitals and similar institutions and, since it is the house of self-undoing, refers to self-inflicted problems.

The houses also retain their usual meanings, for example, the second for possessions, the third for neighbours, etc. One useful feature of the horary chart is that it can be turned. This means that if we want to know something about, for example, the brother of the person to whom the chart refers, we can 'turn' the chart and make the third-house cusp (house of brothers and sisters) the brother's Ascendant. If we want to know about the brother's possessions, we then look at the second house of the turned chart, which is the fourth house of the original chart, and so on.

The ancient planets alone are used as primary significators, with the modern planets providing supplementary information. This means that if Pisces is on a house cusp, its main ruler is Jupiter and not Neptune; similarly Mars for Scorpio and Saturn for Aquarius. No doubt as more research is carried out in this field, the modern planets will play an increasingly important role, but so far not enough work has been done to warrant the use of the more recent rulerships.

In Tom's chart (see Figure 3) the chief significators are: for Tom

– Virgo, Mercury and the Moon; for the illness – Pisces and Jupiter; and for the medicine – Gemini, Mercury and Venus.

Tom is a forty-three-year-old man who has lectured extensively abroad. He has had a great deal of stress over the last few years. There have been several deaths in the family, his wife has cancer, and he has a young child who is fretful and does not sleep well. His job is very demanding and he pushes himself hard. He came complaining of feeling utterly drained at times. His eyes are sunken and he has had a pain in his right side for the last four years. Ten years ago he had a bad attack of fever, with malaria-type symptoms, and he has had seven attacks of varying severity since then. He has had serological tests for malaria, and for many parasitic, bacterial and viral infections. The tests reveal no abnormalities in the blood, but doctors suggest some sort of virus or sore throat. He has a history of exhaustion, neck and shoulder pain, and emotional problems.

The Patient

Mercury, representing Tom, is very strong; he is apparently untouched by everything around him, as it makes no aspects and has no afflictions. Is he trying to weather this whole matter bravely and alone? In describing his problem he constantly refers to survival and refusing to give in to the illness. He admits to liking to be in control of everything around him.

The Moon is applying to the trine of Venus, which suggests that he may need to talk about his difficult situation with a woman, which is perhaps why he is consulting a female practitioner (Venus in Gemini and Mercury in Gemini, ruler of the tenth house of medicine). As Venus rules the ninth house, which is also the third house from the seventh, it could also represent a female neighbour or his wife's sister, in whom he could confide. In fact, it was a woman neighbour, who knows his wife, who insisted that he visit me.

Saturn in the fourth, which is strong, and the irritable Moon conjunct

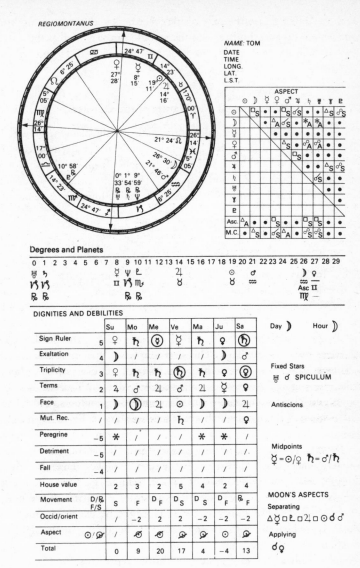

Degrees and Planets

0	1	2	3	4	5	6	7	8	9	10	11	12	13	14	15	16	17	18	19	20	21	22	23	24	25	26	27	28	29

♅ ♄   ☿ ♆ ♇   ♃   ☉   ♂   ☽ ♀

♈ ♈   ♊ ♈ ♏   ♉   ♒   ♒ —

℞ ℞   ℞ ℞   Asc ♊ / ♍ —

DIGNITIES AND DEBILITIES

		Su	Mo	Me	Ve	Ma	Ju	Sa
Sign Ruler	5	♀	♄	☿	☿	♄	♀	♄
Exaltation	4	☽	/	/	/	/	☽	♂
Triplicity	3	♀	♄	♄	♄	♄	♀	☉
Terms	2	♃	♂	♃	♂	♃	☿	♀
Face	1	☽	☽	♃	☉	☽	☽	♃
Mut. Rec.	/	/	/	/	♄	/	/	♀
Peregrine	-5	✳	/	/	/	✳	✳	/
Detriment	-5	/	/	/	/	/	/	/
Fall	-4	/	/	/	/	/	/	/
House value		2	3	2	5	4	2	4
Movement	D/℞ F/S	S	F	D F	D S	D S	D F	℞ F
Occid/orient		/	-2	2	2	-2	-2	-2
Aspect	☉ / ☽	/	☌	☍	☍	☍	☉	☍
Total		0	9	20	17	4	-4	13

Day ☽   Hour ☽

Fixed Stars
♅ ♂ SPICULUM

Antiscions

Midpoints
☿ = ☉/♀   ♄ = ♂/♄

MOON'S ASPECTS
Separating
△☿ ♂ ♇ ☍ ♃ □ ☉ ♂ ♂

Applying
♂ ♀

Figure 3 Tom's decumbiture chart

Mars in the fifth house of children, show his difficult home circumstances. Because Jupiter rules the seventh house as well as the sixth, it may indicate that he is, understandably, affected by his wife's condition.

Part Affected and Nature of the Disease

The disease is shown by the ruler of the sixth and the planet from which the Moon is separating. Jupiter is likely, given the malaria-type infection, to show the blood and liver, and Mars, the planet from which the Moon separates, can show 'corrupted blood'. This is confirmed by Jupiter square Mars. The Moon in air shows the sensitive humour to be blood, as does Mercury in Gemini.

Lilly says that significators in the fiery signs show that a choleric temperament is the problem, and in earthy signs the symptoms are likely to last a long time and come from a melancholy temperament. In airy signs it shows that there is some 'putrefaction' or 'corruption' of the blood, and gouty conditions or certain skin diseases may be present. Watery sign significators show some cold, moist cause.

Lilly gives a table which is based on the premise that a planet in its own sign rules the head. The sign following then rules the throat and neck, and so on down the body to the feet. For example, Mars in its own sign of Aries rules the head. But Mars in Taurus rules the throat and neck, Mars in Gemini the arms and shoulders, and so on until we reach the feet, which are ruled by Mars in Pisces. Similarly, the Sun in Leo will rule the head, whereas the Sun in Virgo will rule the throat. Where a planet rules two signs, the head will be ruled by that planet in both signs. For example, since Mars also rules Scorpio, Mars in Scorpio also rules the head. A glance at the table will show, therefore, that under Mars in Aries two parts of the body are mentioned – not only the head, as might be expected, but also the belly, which belongs to the sequence beginning with Mars in Scorpio.

Under Lilly's system, Jupiter in Taurus represents the shoulders, arms, neck and belly. Tom suffers from stiffness and strain in these areas, and has a pain in the belly.

Left or Right Side of the Body

The left side of the body is considered to be feminine, the right masculine. The upper part of the chart, that 'above the earth' – houses seven, eight, nine, ten, eleven and twelve – are masculine, while the houses 'below the earth' – one, two, three, four, five and six – are feminine. The diurnal signs, those of fire and air, represent the front of the body, and the nocturnal signs, those of earth and water, represent the back.

If the significator of the disease is unfortunate and in a masculine sign, that is, fire or air, above the earth, and afflicted by one or more masculine planets, it shows that the problem lies in the right side of the body, towards the front.

Likewise, if the disease significator is in a feminine sign, in aspect to a feminine planet in a feminine house, the disease is on the left side of the body, towards the back.

Where the matter is not as clearcut as this, and usually it is not, then an assessment of the relative strengths and weaknesses must be made.

The upper part of the body area in question is affected if the planet is only a few degrees into the sign, the middle section if in the middle of the sign, and the lower part if the planet is towards the end of the sign.

Jupiter is above the earth in Tom's chart, in aspect to two masculine planets, and in a nocturnal sign, therefore the problem is on the right, towards the back, and halfway down the area in question – the liver.

The Practitioner

Jupiter, ruler of the sixth house, is also ruler of the seventh and represents not only his wife, but also me, the practitioner, and the picture is a remarkably accurate one. I am shown here as very weak. Jupiter (me) is on the cusp of the ninth house, the house of astrology and publishing, etc. I am writing an astrology book, exhausted and greatly weakened by trying to do too much, wondering if perhaps I had not really bitten off more than I could chew (Jupiter!) and feeling burnt out (Jupiter combust!). In fact, on the evening of Tom's appointment I

Table 9. Lilly's table of parts of the body related to planets in signs

	♄	♃	♂	☉	♀	☿	☽
♈	breast arm	neck throat heart belly	belly head	thighs	kidneys feet	reproductive organs legs	knees head
♉	heart breast belly	shoulders arms neck belly	kidneys throat	knees	sex organs head	thighs feet	legs throat
♊	belly heart	breast kidneys sex organs	sex organs arms breast	legs ankles	thighs throat	knees head	feet shoulders arms thighs
♋	kidneys belly sex organs	heart sex organs thighs	feet	knees shoulders arms	knees shoulders arms	legs throat eyes	head breast stomach
♌	sex organs kidneys	belly thighs knees	knees heart belly	head	legs breast heart	feet arms shoulders throat	throat stomach heart
♍	thighs sex organs feet	kidneys knees	legs belly	throat	feet stomach heart belly	head breast heart	arms shoulders bowels
♎	knees thighs	sex organs legs head eyes	feet kidneys sex organs	shoulders arms	head small intestines	throat heart stomach belly	breast kidneys heart belly
♏	knees legs	thighs feet	head sex organs arms thighs	breast heart	throat kidneys sex organs	shoulders arms bowels back	stomach heart sex organs belly
♐	legs feet	knees head thighs	throat thighs hands feet	heart belly	shoulders arms sex organs thighs	breast kidneys heart sex organs	bowels thighs back
♑	head feet	legs neck eyes knees	arms shoulders knees legs	belly back	breast heart thighs	stomach heart sex organs	kidneys knees thighs
♒	neck head	feet arms shoulders breast	breast legs heart	kidneys sex organs	heart knees heart	bowels thighs ankles	sex organs legs
♓	arms shoulders neck	head breast heart	heart feet belly ankles	sex organs thighs	belly legs neck throat	kidneys knees sex organs thighs	thighs feet

was giving a talk away from home, and arrived back so ill that I had to go to bed for two days, literally unable to move. If the chart is turned to look at my sixth house – the twelfth of the radical (original) chart – the significator of my illness is Mercury, in 'my' third house of communications. Too much writing, talking and rushing about had made me ill. The ruler of my tenth house, the house of medicine and the fourth of the radical chart, is Jupiter – myself. Physician heal thyself? I did, at least temporarily, with a complete banishment of all stimuli (Mercury) – no phone–calls, books, noise, movement or even thought.

The lord of the hour also influences the patient–practitioner relationship. If Saturn is lord of the house in the decumbiture chart, the patient is likely to have a long illness. Where Mars is the hour ruler, the patient may be cantankerous, uncharitable and uncooperative towards the practitioner. Jupiter or Venus represents a happier relationship, and it usually means that the practitioner will be praised and well-rewarded financially, even if the patient does not get well. Perhaps we should arrange our appointment books accordingly!

Prognosis and Speed of Recovery

The course and outcome of the problem can be assessed by examining the relative strengths of the significators of the patient and those of the disease. The following aphorisms of William Lilly show that the assessment may be far from straightforward.

If the significators of the patient are well-aspected, unafflicted and stronger, then the illness will be thrown off in a short time. If the disease significators are stronger, and especially if they are in fixed signs, it indicates that the illness will be of long duration and hard to resolve.

> The Sun gives short diseases.
> The Moon's tend to be recurrent.
> Mercury's are changeable.
> Venus brings problems which are neither too long nor too violent.
> Mars's diseases are short and violent.
> Jupiter's are short.
> Saturn tends to chronic disorders.

If the sign on the sixth is fixed, the illness is likely to be a long one; if it is cardinal, of short duration; and if mutable, neither short nor protracted, but the symptoms will change often, the patient sometimes feeling better, sometimes worse, before it runs its course.

If the Moon is in a fixed sign, there will be a long illness; if in a cardinal, a short one, and if in a mutable, then in between and change-able.

Where the Moon is conjuncting a planet which is oriental, direct and swift, a short illness can be expected. Where the planet is occidental or retrograde, the opposite is the case.

If the ruler of the sixth is retrograde, combust, in the eighth or twelfth house, and either square, conjunct or in opposition to Mars, Saturn or the ruler of the eighth or the fourth, it can presage a long and difficult illness.

Bringing all these factors together gives a mixed picture of Tom's condition. Arguing for a short illness is the sheer strength of Mercury, as well as the fact that Jupiter usually indicates brevity. On the other hand, both the Moon and Jupiter are in fixed signs. The Moon is conjuncting Mars, which is occidental. As Mars is regarded as a malefic planet and seems to be the cause of the problem, this makes matters worse. Mutable Pisces on the sixth-house cusp promises a fluctuating course, but the very fact that the root problem has been going on for ten years makes it unlikely that this will clear up overnight.

Critical Days

The Moon is used to follow the course of acute illnesses. The days on which the Moon is at 45, 90, 135 and 180 degrees from its position in the decumbiture chart are called critical days, in which a change in the patient's condition can be expected. The nature of the aspects the Moon makes on these days, and with which planets, will show whether the condition is improving or becoming worse.

If the illness is very acute, a week may be too long to wait for the first critical day or half crisis to occur (at 45 degrees) in order to discover what is happening. If that is the case, the indicative days are used. This is where the Moon has transited $22\frac{1}{2}$ degrees (or multiples of that figure) from its decumbiture position. Again the aspects made by the

Moon are examined. In addition, the days that the Moon transits the cusps of the sixth, seventh and eighth houses are noted, as well as the nature of the aspects and the planets involved.

When the transiting Moon conjuncts, squares or opposes the decumbiture Moon, the ruler of the sixth, any planet in the sixth, or a planet afflicting the Ascendant or the Ascendant ruler, the patient's condition will deteriorate.

A sextile or trine of the Moon, however, to the ruler of the Ascendant, or to the rulers of the signs on the cusps of the ninth, tenth and eleventh houses, will bring an amelioration. This is also the case when the ruler of the Ascendant makes a good aspect to the Sun, provided the latter is not adversely involved in the disease.

Tom is suffering from a chronic condition and therefore the Sun is used as an indicator instead of the Moon. Its position 45, 90, 135 and 180 degrees further on from its decumbiture position is noted, as well as the aspects it makes to the other planets. These are the critical days. The indicative days are calculated and used in the same way as with the Moon, that is, to take an intermediate check.

In this case, at the half crisis, when the Sun is in Leo, it conjuncts the Moon and trines both Mars and Saturn. At the full crisis, in Scorpio, it conjuncts Pluto. Next, in Aquarius, it squares Jupiter. Finally, when back again in Taurus, it trines Saturn. This case clearly needs to be carefully monitored at those times.

Therapeutic Measures

The seventeenth-century herbalist, Nicholas Culpeper, gives the following guidelines for the use of remedies in his classic work, *Culpeper's Complete Herbal*:

1. Fortify the body with herbs of the nature of the Lord of the Ascendant, 'tis no matter whether he be a Fortune or Infortune in this case.
2. Let your medicine be something antipathetical to the Lord of the Sixth.
3. Let your medicine be something of the nature of the sign ascending.

4. If the Lord of the Tenth be strong make use of his medicines.
5. If this cannot well be make use of the medicines of the Light of Time [that is, the Sun by day and the Moon by night].
6. Be sure always to fortify the grieved part of the body by sympathetical remedies.
7. Regard the heart, keep that upon the wheels, because the Sun is the foundation of life, and therefore those universal remedies *Aurum Potabile*, and the philosopher's stone cure all diseases by fortifying the heart.

Mercury herbs are indicated immediately in Tom's case, as Mercury is so strong and rules both the Ascendant and Midheaven, which is itself strong. Valerian is a good choice and, as it is hot in the first degree and dry in the second, does not provide too much heat. (These qualities are discussed in Chapter 7, see page 158). Heat is to be avoided as Mars, the planet afflicting the Moon, shows that the disease is hot. Not only that, but Jupiter, which is usually sanguine by temperament, is heated up as it is combust with the Sun. Mercury medicines are antipathetical to Jupiter, lord of the sixth.

The best remedies for the grieved parts of the body are dandelion and dock, which cleanse the blood and liver. They are both ruled by Jupiter, and are cold and dry in the second degree. The expulsion of choler requires herbs sympathetic to the gall-bladder (Mars), such as gentian or barberry bark, but again only small quantities are needed as they engender heat.

Tom's case was not chosen to show the therapeutic excellence of this method. Almost any other case history would have done that better, especially as the outcome is to date uncertain, owing to the prolonged nature of the illness. (Nor does it show me in a particularly flattering light!) It was selected because it provides an unusually clear and uncomplicated demonstration of decumbiture technique. In reality, most charts are far less straightforward than this one, and a great deal of weighing and balancing of the various factors is required before coming to any judgement.

REFERENCES

Culpeper, Nicholas, *Culpeper's Astrological Judgement of Diseases*, London, 1655

Culpeper, Nicholas, *Culpeper's Complete Herbal and English Physician Enlarged*, Richard Evans, London, 1815

Ebertin, Reinhold, *The Combination of Stellar Influences*, American Foundation of Astrologers, Monroe, 1972

Lilly, William, *Christian Astrology*, 1647. Reprinted Regulus Facsimile Editions, London, 1985

Lorenz, Maries, *Tools of Astrology*, Omega Press, Topanga, California, ud

Ptolemy, *Tetrabiblios*, Loeb Classical Library, William Heinemann, London, 1980

Further Reading

Barclay, Olivia, *Horary Correspondence Course*, Mongeham Lodge Cottage, Great Mongeham, Deal, Kent

Watters, Barbara, *Horary Astrology and the Judgement of Events*, Valhalla Books, Washington, 1982

6

THE THERAPEUTIC
SITUATION

Like any other therapeutic encounter, the astrological consultation has its own special set of structures and dynamics. I do not want to do more than touch on a few of these here as there are already some excellent books on the subject (see the reference section at the end of the chapter). Maritha Pottenger's *Healing with the Horoscope*, in particular, contains a wealth of factual information, while the books edited by Marcus Lefébure give some moving intellectual and spiritual insights. The 'Counselling in Action' books, published by Sage Publications, are a series of high-quality, practical guides to counselling. Especially recommended is *Person-Centred Counselling in Action* by Dave Mearns and Brian Thorpe. The Faculty of Astrological Studies now also offers post-diploma counselling courses and has an impressive line-up of tutors and consultants. The Centre for Psychological Astrology in London provides a professional training programme which must be unique in the range, depth and quality of the material it presents. The workshops are led by world-class experts in their own fields.

A basic awareness of the importance of the therapeutic setting, personal qualities, interpersonal skills, and the mechanisms of projection and counter-projection is vital for anyone who is using astrology as part of the healing process, for these factors can make or break the effectiveness of the treatment. It is important, too, for us to set some objectives and personal guidelines, as without them it is difficult, if not impossible to assess the quality of our work and to take steps to improve it. Five factors that should be taken into consideration are the astrologer, the client, the relationship between them, the therapy session and the stages of therapy.

THE ASTROLOGER

It is important to know what we are offering and what we are aiming at in working professionally with clients and patients.

The first question that needs to be asked is – what is a medical astrologer? It is obviously someone who is competent in astrology, but what about the medical aspect? Does the person also have to have a medical background or training in some kind of therapy? My answer would be that, while it would obviously be advantageous, it is not essential. What is important, and ethical, is to do only what we have the expertise to do. There are many ways of helping people towards health. Most psychological astrologers are in fact already involved in healing work, in that they are able to put clients in touch with their own wholeness, which equals health.

Probably the most satisfying way an astrologer with no medical training can operate in the healing professions is as a key member of the therapeutic team. This is how several prominent medical astrologers work, among them Simon Duindam of the Asclepios School of Medical Astrology in the Netherlands. To quote Duindam: 'What I do as a medical astrologer is to clear up – after the diagnoses are made by physicians – the mental-psychic patterns that are related to this or that particular disease, and then refer the patient to experts who are able to give the necessary treatment. I believe this is a responsible way of working.'

Astrologers with a clear understanding of the basic medical sciences of anatomy, physiology and pathology, or of Ayurvedic or Chinese medicine are able to follow the dis-ease processes from their beginnings at an inner level to their manifestation at the physical level, and to trace the actions of the planets throughout the body. These associations are still only tentative as yet, and there is some fascinating work waiting to be done in this field.

Those who are also trained in one of the healing arts have the advantage of being able not only to treat the patient in a more comprehensive way, but to apply the astrological language of symbols to their own speciality, which makes the process doubly challenging and rewarding.

It is generally accepted that astrologers are unable to interpret charts beyond the reaches of their own knowledge, understanding and wisdom. It is therefore imperative that astrologers with any degree of pride in their craft, in addition to improving their knowledge and skills, work at refining and polishing that most crucial tool of their profession – themselves. This, for a medical astrologer especially, needs to be carried out at all levels – physical, intellectual, emotional and spiritual – to allow the greatest possible understanding and empathy with the client/patient.

THE CLIENT

Most clients have only a very hazy idea of what astrology has to offer, and that is usually wrong. This is hardly surprising, considering the garbled nonsense that the popular press disseminates. I find it is essential to be very open and clear at the outset about what is being offered, otherwise there are likely to be endless misunderstandings and false expectations which get in the way of the work. If there is no clarity about objectives, then there can be no sense of satisfaction of having reached, or at least approached them. I will not accept any clients until they have read my information sheet, which states very plainly what I do and, just as important, do not offer.

The motivations of patients/clients who come for treatment are varied. Some are genuinely determined to get well and are willing to do anything which is necessary to achieve this. Some would quite like to recover and are happy to go along with some of the measures, provided it does not involve too great an inconvenience. Some are not yet ready or able to relinquish their illness, but come along out of a sense of duty, for if one is ill one 'should' get treatment, shouldn't one? Yet others come, having been to therapists the length and breadth of the land, to prove once again that they are incurable. I feel that it is important to respect the patients' wishes/needs – whose life is it after all? – and not to insist insensitively that they get well. Other practitioners have disagreed with me, but I believe that ultimately all we can do is to provide the most favourable conditions for healing, share our knowledge and experience joyfully, and use our skills to the best of our ability and integrity in each case, suspending all judgements and expectations. The rest is out of our hands. There may or may not be, in each patient's life, a time to heal, and it is a privilege rather than our right if that time happens to coincide with a visit to our practice.

Healing work of any value is always a two-way process, and the therapist's own wounded areas will inevitably be exposed. For this reason therapists need to base their work on a solid foundation; the experience of psychological and spiritual processes, and considerable self-knowledge, maturity and dispassion are required in order to cope not only with the client's pain, but with their own, which is often touched simultaneously. There are no coincidences, and astrologers often experience, with wry amusement, a stream of clients presenting problems not so very far removed from their own. One of the great advantages of astrology is that, with the aid of synastry techniques and the decumbiture chart, it is possible to look at the interpersonal issues between the client and the astrologer/therapist. With these insights the sting can be taken out of many problems that arise. I tend, however, not to check the synastry closely unless things start to get difficult, partly because there is usually no time for anything that is not essential, and partly because I feel it can get in the way of concentrating on the patient, whose time it is after all.

In interpreting clients' charts we are not simply handing over impersonal information. We are touching the very core of their being. Astrology is a sacred art, and an astrological session is religious in the deepest sense of the word – it helps reconnect that person with their own and the greater wholeness. It is a situation which has potential for great healing or great destruction, especially as clients are generally rather overawed at first by what they perceive as the oracular nature of astrology.

A wrong word or insinuation can have devastating effects, leaching out acid over the years into a person's psyche. Most clients, of course, are selective listeners and will latch on to what they want to hear, either positive or negative, and are perfectly capable of believing, even insisting, that an astrologer has said something which in fact they have not. Recording each session on audio cassette tape can help to overcome that problem.

In order to make the most of the healing potential, the atmosphere of the session needs to be one in which the client can trust enough to be as open as possible, with no sense of being judged or pushed. George Eliot's description of friendship illustrates this quality: 'Friendship is the comfort, the inexpressible comfort, of feeling safe with a person, having neither to weigh thoughts, nor measure words but pouring all right out just as they are, chaff and grain together, certain that a faithful hand will take and sift them, keep what is worth keeping, and with a breath of comfort, blow the rest away.'

As astrology cannot be practised in a spiritual vacuum, the astrologer also needs to have come consciously to some sort of conclusions, even if they are only provisional, about such issues as fate and free will, the meaning of illness and the purpose of life. These conclusions have a powerful influence on the direction, value judgements and quality of an astrologer's work. If they are not acknowledged, internally if not externally, it can lead to misunderstandings at best, and covert (or even blatant) missionary manipulation at worst. It is usually helpful to give clients a brief résumé of the frame of reference which is being used, so that they can (and indeed they should be actively encouraged to) translate it into their own philosophical terms, which are bound to be different from those of the astrologer. There are as many ways of interpreting the universe as there are individuals, and each way is valid if it makes life meaningful for that person.

Like any other tool, astrology can be used inappropriately and can even get in the way of therapy. One of the gifts of astrology is that it provides an objective map of subjective reality. This often gives clients the information and necessary distance from their own situation, so that they have a measure of choice and control over whether or not they remain in whatever situation they find themselves. Taken too far, this can lead the astrologer and client to being caught in the head trap of playing about with intellectual explanations. Talking *about* the chart rather than living it, after a certain point, is counter-productive, in that it cuts off both client and astrologer from experiencing the immediacy of the subjective reality and can spell therapeutic death.

THE STAGES OF THERAPY

The exercises below can be used on those who are basically psychologically healthy and stable. Anyone who is not needs professional help from a trained psychotherapist or psychiatrist. (The function of the astrologer in that type of case is to translate the astrological information for those practitioners, assuming that they are receptive.) I divide the stages of therapy into identification, exploration and upgrading.

Identification

The first essential is locate and define the problem areas. This can be achieved fairly easily using standard astrological techniques and some of the methods found in other chapters of this book. The main function of medical astrology, as has been emphasized elsewhere, is not to provide a medical diagnosis, but to identify and treat the root causes. The underlying premise here is that by dealing with the problems 'upstream', in the psyche, it can have a sparing effect on the body.

Exploration

After the initial session the first question a client usually asks is, 'But what can I *do* about it?' The first impulse is to want to jump in immediately to try to change by willpower and force 'unacceptable' and painful patterns of behaviour into those which the conscious part of the client finds pleasing. This actually amounts to a rape of one part of the psyche by another and can only be done at our own peril. Until a situation is acknowledged and known intimately, it cannot be dealt with constructively. The greater our knowledge and sensitivity to our psychological patterns, the less power they have over us. Awareness means no longer being chained to the wheel of fate, or blindly propelled by our own unconscious, but being actively on the path to self-fulfilment. So the next necessary step, prior to trying to change anything, is to attempt to understand it.

One of the first things I ask many clients to do is to keep a special notebook and to note down the situations in which they find themselves indulging in the type of behaviour linked to whatever particular chart feature is under review. Making judgements on the behavioural pattern is absolutely forbidden. They are asked simply to look, as if they were outside observers reporting on an incident. They are to carry on with the activity whenever it arises spontaneously, for a specified length of time, usually a month, but to do it in full consciousness, not stopping it in any way. After a while they may be asked to exaggerate their actions, to actively encourage them, and to observe what happens. Even these simple exercises can be extraordinarily effective in breaking seemingly compulsive behaviour.

There are many methods of probing further. Clients can take specific examples of where the same or similar situations were prominent in the past and describe them. This can be done through whatever medium of communication the client finds most appropriate – either verbally, in writing, or through drawings, sculpture or even sound, movement or dance. It is useful to trace the history of what happened when the problem area was activated by transits, especially of the heavy planets, to see if a pattern can be identified.

Clients with a strong Virgo or Gemini emphasis generally enjoy Progoff's Intensive Journal approach to exploration. This is an aid to self-understanding and therapy where expression through writing, using a specially structured journal, is the main therapeutic tool. Gestalt exercises, where clients re-enact and rescript old events and patterns, may also be helpful.

In *The Development of the Personality*, Howard Sasportas makes the suggestion, which I have found valuable, of turning interpretations of chart features into personal statements. Instead of saying, for example, Sun square Saturn means that the creative energy is blocked, the client makes it into a statement of a belief that they have incorporated into their life. It could be something like 'my father disapproves of me', or 'life is hard'. The next stage is to expand on that one point by writing about it or giving a lecture on it.

Astrodrama is another good way of getting to know more about the interplay of planetary energies. Guided imagery and active imagination may also be employed, using astrological symbolism appropriate to the planet or planets involved. Cherry Gilchrist's book, *Planetary Symbolism*, provides many useful ideas and starting points for this type of work. However, some personal experience of psychosynthesis, psychodrama or transpersonal psychology is virtually essential before these methods can be used effectively.

Upgrading

The next step is to find new, more creative ways of expressing difficult chart features. It is not by concentrating on what is wrong with us, necessary though that stage is, that we become healthy in the full sense of the word. It is by living with joy with what is *right* with us and by embracing who we are. I have often found that problematic aspects become much less problematic simply by knowing about them. It is as if they lose a lot of their power when exposed to the light, and in some cases new, more spontaneous and healthy behaviour patterns fall into place without any special extra effort. Liz Greene has said of Pluto that we cannot change it, but what we can change is our attitude towards it. I believe this to be true of all the planets. We cannot brook the urgency of the planetary energies to express themselves in our lives, any more than King Canute could hold back the waves. We can *try* to resist them, or attempt to harness their energies to serve our own ego desires – but that is where most of the problems arise in the first place. Or we can honour them and co-operate in trying to find a place for their highest and purest expressions. Frequently this latter course will run counter to our conscious wishes, but it leads to growth and richness beyond measure. As Epictetus said: 'Seek not to have things happen as you choose them, but rather choose them to happen as they do, and so shall you live prosperously.'

So what is to be changed and upgraded, then, is not the planetary energies themselves, but our relationship to them. The important point is that any new patterns that are cultivated *must* allow a natural expression of the chart features under consideration. A fir tree is not an apple tree, and trying to force it to become one not only insults the fir tree but, by denying its true nature and needs, will eventually deform and destroy it.

As well as changing our attitude to what is being expressed through us, another positive step is to find more appropriate outlets for these energies. There are obviously situations that are more favourable to certain types of planetary energies than others.

Charles Harvey gives a good example of this in his essay 'Ideal

Astrology', published in *The Future of Astrology*, edited by A. T. Mann. Writing about the potential of Sun square Mars, he refers to the Churchill Sailing Schooner Scheme for delinquent adolescents. There it has been found that the wildest tearways are often the ones who become heroes, showing remarkable leadership potential when battling against the elements. Circumstances in which energies can be allowed to express freely and constructively are healing.

A useful way of providing role models for upgrading is in looking at the charts of other people who have the same configurations and who have coped well with life. I have only hard aspects to the Sun and it was enormously reassuring to note that Jung, a particular hero of mine, had this too. One of the traditional delineations of this feature is that these natives will, with such afflictions, make nothing of their lives. By having living proof of the constructive potential of particular chart features we can begin to thumb our noses at the more negative expectations, both external and internal. In his book *The Astrological Aspects*, Charles Carter discusses each of the planetary combinations and cites prominent people who had either harmonious or inharmonious contacts or the conjunctions. Unfortunately some of the celebrities mentioned are no longer widely known nowadays, and Pluto is not included as it had not been discovered when the book was written. Despite these drawbacks it is a first-class source of 'role model' material. It is often useful to find out the client's own heroes to see if there are any chart similarities which can be worked on. The Astrological Association Data Section has a wealth of birth information both on the famous and the infamous.

Using keywords, new and more positive statements can be made about the planetary combinations. For example, those with a Sun–Saturn contact might say, 'I am a responsible person, capable of manifesting my creativity concretely in the world, using setbacks as valuable lessons on the way'. These statements can be used as affirmations. The one proviso is that the affirmation is a realistic statement of the aspect involved. It would be quite absurd, for example, for a Sun–Saturn person to pronounce, 'Life is joyful; there are no problems!'

Literature and art that describes the combination of planetary energies in a positive way can be inspiring, comforting and strengthening. I have always enjoyed collecting fragments of prose and poetry that have moved me. They have proved invaluable as resource material to give to patients as 'food' for the journey until they stock up on their own.

One of the most impressive examples of allowing a higher expression of energies is in the work of Alcoholics Anonymous. The negative Neptunian/Pisces behaviour of the drunk is transformed into compassionate, devoted service to fellow-sufferers and reliance on a greater power. The A A handbook, *Twelve Steps and Twelve Traditions*, is a useful guide not only for alcoholics, but for anyone interested in upgrading work.

Planetary energies do not always have to be expressed through behaviour patterns. Sport is a particularly good outlet for taking the edge off many of the hard aspects, but it must be an activity which relates closely to the symbolism, and, just as important, also appeals to the client. For example, karate is excellent for Mars in aspect to Saturn, as it demands the disciplined use of force. A Venus–Mars contact might use fencing to express its grace, aggression and flirtation. Or belly-dancing, which demands the energetic, but seductive use of muscles. Dynamic meditation, which aims at stilling the mind by noisy and strenuous exertion, might suit Mars–Neptune. The permutations are endless.

The most common non-psychological activity for disturbed relationships between planetary energies, however, is in the giving and taking of medicines, and this is the subject of the next chapter.

REFERENCES

Alcoholics Anonymous, *Twelve Steps and Twelve Traditions*, A.A. General Service Office, York, 1987

Carter, Charles, *The Astrological Aspects*, L. N. Fowler & Co., Romford, 1981

Duindam, Simon, 'Medical Astrology: A Case Study' in *The Astrological Journal*, July/August, 1988

Gilchrist, Cherry, *Planetary Symbolism*, Saros Foundation, Astrological Association of Great Britain, London, 1980

Greene, Liz, and Sasportas, Howard, *The Development of the Personality*, Routledge Kegan Paul, London, 1987

Lefebure, M., *Conversations on Counselling*, T. & T. Clark, Edinburgh, 1982

Lefebure, M., *Human Experience and the Art of Counselling*, T. & T. Clark, Edinburgh, 1985

Mann, A. T. (ed.), *The Future of Astrology*, Unwin Hyman, London, 1987

Mearns, David, and Thorpe, Brian, *Person-Centred Counselling in Action*, Sage Publications, London, 1988

Pottenger, Maritha, *Healing with the Horoscope, a Guide to Counselling*, ACS Publications, San Diego, 1982

Progoff, Ira, *At a Journal Workshop*, Dialogue House, USA 1986

Further Reading

Arroyo, Stephen, *The Practice and Profession of Astrology*, CRCS Publications, Reno, Nevada, 1984

Greene, Liz, and Sasportas, Howard, *Dynamics of the Unconscious*, Samuel Weiser, York Beach, Maine, 1988

Rose, Christina, *Astrological Counselling*, Aquarian Press, Wellingborough, 1982

Rosenblum, Bernard, *The Astrologer's Guide to Counselling*, CRCS Publications, Reno, Nevada, 1983

7

MATERIA MEDICA

A medicine can have one of three functions. It can assist, resist or balance processes taking place in the body. One of the perennial debates in medicine is whether it is better to assist nature's attempts to heal or to intervene actively.

The doctrine of contraries states that medicine should be of an opposite nature to the symptoms of the disease. Modern orthodox medical practice is based almost entirely on this belief. It really comes into its own and is unrivalled in dealing with a small number of acute, life-threatening conditions. It has, however, a poor track record in relieving chronic problems. There is a good argument for intervention when the patient appears to be endangered. An example of this might be a small child with a very high temperature and a history of fever-induced convulsions. Normally a fever is an excellent sign that the body's defence mechanisms are working well, but here they may be working too well, to the extent of damaging the patient in the process. In this case it would seem sensible to tone down the reaction to within safe limits.

The opposite approach is to use measures that are of the same nature as the disease process. These are the sympathetic remedies. Examples of this approach are homoeopathy, in which it is maintained that 'like cures like', and in the realm of psychology, Viktor Frankl's use of paradoxical intention, where the client, instead of trying to resist psychological symptoms, embraces them and actively encourages the process.

In native American Indian medicine, and in the European doctrine of signatures, the shape and colour as well as the habitat of a plant is important in assessing its medicinal qualities. The habitat, especially, shows which natural difficulties the species has learned to overcome and adapt to, and the conditions in which it flourishes. Each plant can therefore be seen as holding the quintessence of a particular challenge of nature that has been successfully resolved. Where a person is faced with a challenging situation, either emotionally or physically, ingesting a plant which 'knows' how to survive and thrive in these conditions can teach the sufferer, at a deep level, how to do so too.

According to that tradition, for example, where a person is going through a period of sour, acid feelings, and/or whose body tissues tend to acidity, taking plants which are native to acid soil will be helpful. It is interesting that many of the plants that grow in sour moorlands are used predominantly for arthritic and urinary problems, both of which have associations with excessive acidity.

An example of the third method, that of balancing the processes taking place in the body, is found in Ayurvedic medicine which, among many other techniques, uses foods to increase or decrease under- or over-activity. The use of nutritional and hormonal supplements is an allopathic equivalent.

Where there is an excess of any factor, say air, this implies an imbalance of the other elements too. This can be compensated, without interfering with the underlying process, by using foods and remedies that provide the qualities of fire, which is generally low when air is high. Earth and water remedies could be given as well, if these were indicated.

In *The English Physician Enlarged*, Culpeper says: 'Consider, that all diseases are cured by their contraries, but all parts of the body maintained by their likes: then if heat be the cause of the disease, give the cold medicine appropriated to it.' His rules for treating conditions astrologically are discussed more fully in Chapter 5.

Figure 4 shows the traditional rulers of the houses. By looking at the houses, it can be seen at a glance which planets naturally oppose each other. By extension, the diagram can be used to find antipathetical remedies. If, for example, an illness is caused by Jupiter, this would be treated with a Mercury remedy, and not one ruled by Saturn as might be expected. Similarly, Saturn remedies counteract conditions caused by the Moon and the Sun.

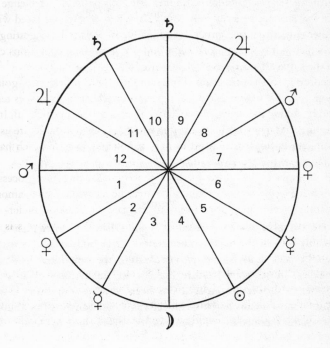

Figure 4 The traditional house rulerships

Some commonly held associations with the planets and signs are given below.

Sun

Sun remedies strengthen, especially the heart and the immune system.

Many Sun herbs are effective against allergies and are mildly diaphoretic, that is, they induce sweating, which both gives a sensation of heat and throws off toxins through the skin.

Moon

Moon remedies are generally cooling. Some work on the lymphatic system, some are alteratives (promoting a positive change in the vital functions), while others are emetics (producing vomiting).

Mercury

The main Mercury remedies are the nervines. These 'feed', tone and soothe the nervous system. As an over-active Mercury causes excitement and wind, many Mercury remedies are anti-flatulent carminatives.

Venus

There are more remedies ruled by Venus than any other planet, presumably because the main requirement of a sick body or soul is that it is brought back into harmony. Venus rules the amphoteric balancing remedies, those which restore the correct functioning of an organ, whether it be over- or under-active. Because of its connection with the kidneys, most Venus herbs, as indeed most herbs anyway, are diuretics. The soothing remedies – the demulcents – also belong to Venus.

Mars

As might be expected, the hot fiery remedies are ruled by Mars. These range from the stimulants to the rubefacients (from the Latin 'make red') right through to the caustics, which raise blisters and burn. Surgery and cauterization also come under Mars.

Jupiter

Jupiter remedies are restorative and antispasmodic. Many of them are anthelmintic, that is, they remove worms. Reflecting Jupiter's connection with the liver, the alexipharmics (poison antidotes) so beloved of medieval writers belong here too. When reading old herbals it is easy to gain the impression that poisoning from the bites of mad dogs and scorpions were once everyday occurrences!

Saturn

Saturn cools and constricts and therefore rules the anti-inflammatory, anti-pyretic (fever-reducing) and astringent remedies.

Uranus

Electrical and vibrational therapies belong to Uranus. Two of the best known are the electric shock treatment, and the resuscitation of people suffering a heart attack using a strong electric current. Electric shock treatment for depression and mental illness has had a bad press recently, but certain doctors speak of impressive results too. Some recent research seems to indicate that it depends on the part of the brain stimulated as to whether the effect is pleasant and healing or produces catastrophic feelings. Right-brain stimulation is implicated in the negative effects and that of the left in positive ones, which further confirms the research detailed in Chapter 2 (see page 15). Astrologically Uranus rules rhythmus and electricity. Electric shock to both the brain and heart seems to re-introduce aligned pulsation to these organs by the principle of entrain-ment.

Neptune

Neptune is connected with altered states of sensation and consciousness, and its remedies are the analgesics, the hypnotics and anaesthetics. Suggestion and hypnosis are also Neptunian.

Pluto

Antibiotics – those remedies which kill some forms of life in order to save others – radio-active treatments and those medicines used in cancer chemotherapy belong to Pluto's domain. These are drastic measures, not to be used lightly. Amputation is ruled by Pluto (and Mars), especially if it is followed by fitting an artificial substitute (prosthesis). Organ transplants also relate to this symbolism.

This is probably the oldest form of medicine and it has long been used in conjunction with astrology. A few of the most common herbs are listed below, together with their rulerships and qualities. Most of the information comes from Culpeper's *An English Physician Enlarged*.

Remedies are either hot, cold, dry or moist, a categorization which is found in traditional Greek, Arab and European medicine. The quality describes the effect of the substance on the body. There are four degrees of each quality. The first degree is the most mild, while the fourth degree is the strongest. The human body is hot in the first degree, owing to its natural heat, therefore medicines which are hot in the first degree are the most gentle and closest to the body's own nature. Where the illness has a cold cause, hot medicines are called for, and where the cause is hot, then cooler ones should be used. However, cold medicines should not be used for a prolonged period as they are antagonistic to the nature of the body.

There is clearly a great deal of work to be done by astrologers who are also herbalists, as some of the rulerships seem, at first glance anyway, inappropriate. There are also many plants with rulerships shared by two or more planets. Dylan Warren-Davis has carried out some excellent research work in this field and has, *inter alia*, written a scholarly treatise on the connections between willow and the Moon.

Herbs of the Sun

Sun plants have yellowish or reddish flowers, smell and taste pleasant, and grow majestically. They prefer open and sunny places.

> Angelica (*Angelica archangelica*) – hot and dry in the third
> Centaury (*Centaurium erythraea*) – hot and dry in the second
> Chamomile (*Matricaria recutita*) – hot and dry in the first
> Eyebright (*Euphrasia spp.*) – hot and dry in the first

Juniper berries (*Juniperus communis*) – hot in the third, dry in the first

Marigold (*Calendula officinalis*) – hot in the second, moist in the first

Rosemary (*Rosmarinus officinalis*) – hot and dry in the second

Rue (*Ruta graveolens*) – hot and dry in the third

Saffron (*Crocus sativus*) – hot in the second, dry in the first

Sun foods are rice (hot in the first, dry in the second), sunflowers, grapes and walnuts.

Herbs of the Moon

Moon plants have thick, juicy leaves and a watery or sweetish taste. They like to grow in damp places or by water.

Chickweed (*Stellaria media*) – cold in the second, moist in the fourth

Cleavers (*Galium aparine*) – hot and dry in the first

White willow (*Salix alba*) – cold and dry in the second

Moon foods are cabbages, the cresses, cucumber (cold and moist in the second), lettuce (cold in the second, moist in the fourth), melons (cold and moist in the second) and pumpkins.

Herbs of Mercury

Mercury herbs like sandy, barren places; their flowers may be of almost any colour or even multicoloured. Their seeds are usually carried in husks or pods.

Aniseed (*Pimpinella anisum*) – hot and dry in the third

Dill (*Anethum graveolens*) – hot and dry in the second

Elecampane (*Inula helenium*) – hot and dry in the third

Fennel (*Foeniculum vulgare*) – hot and dry in the second

Horehound (*Marrubium vulgare*) – hot in the second, dry in the third

Lavender (*Lavandula officinalis*) – hot in the third, dry in the second

Liquorice (*Glycyrrhiza glabra*) – hot and moist in the first

Marjoram (*Origanum marjorana*) – hot and dry in the second
Parsley (*Petroselinum crispum*) – hot and dry in the second
Southernwood (*Artemisia abrotanum*) – hot and dry in the third
Valerian (*Valeriana officinalis*) – hot in the first, dry in the second
(according to the Greeks), moist (according to the Arabs)

Mercury foods are hazelnuts, beans, mushrooms, fennel and pomegranates.

Herbs of Venus

Venus herbs usually have white flowers, smooth leaves, a sweet taste and a pleasant smell.

Archangel (*Lamium album*) – hot and dry in the second
Burdock herb (*Arctium lappa*) – hot and dry in the first
Burdock root (*Arctium lappa*) – cold and dry in the first
Coltsfoot (*Tussilago farfara*) – cold and dry in the first
Daisy (*Bellis perennis*) – cold in the second, moist in the fourth
Lady's mantle (*Alchemilla vulgaris*) – hot and dry in the second
Marshmallow herb (*Althaea officinalis*) – hot and dry in the first
Marshmallow root (*Althaea officinalis*) – dry in the second
Meadowsweet (*Filipendula ulmaria*) – hot and dry in the third
Mints (e.g. *Mentha piperita*) – hot and dry in the third
Mugwort (*Artemisia vulgaris*) – hot and dry in the second
Pennyroyal (*Mentha pulegium*) – hot and dry in the third
Plantain (*Plantago major*) – cold and dry in the second
Tansy (*Tanacetum vulgare*) – hot in the second, dry in the third
Thyme (*Thymus vulgaris*) – hot and dry in the third
Vervain (*Verbena officinalis*) – hot and dry in the second
Yarrow (*Achillea millefolium*) – cold in the first

Venus foods are beans, brambles, parsnips (temperate and moist), cherries, gooseberries, lentils and plums.

Herbs of Mars

Mars plants are reddish with pointed, sharp leaves and a burning taste. They prefer to grow in dry places.

Agnus castus (*Vitex agnus castus*) – hot in the third
Anemone (*Anemone pulsatilla*) – cold and dry in the second
Broom (*Sarothamnus scoparius*) – hot and dry in the second
Bryony (*Bryonia dioica and alba*) – hot and dry in the third
Garlic (*Allium sativum*) – hot and dry in the fourth
Ginger (*Zingiber officinale*) – hot and dry in the third
Hops (*Humulus lupulus*) – hot and dry in the second
Mustard seed (*Sinapis alba*) – hot and dry in the third
Nettles (*Urtica dioica* and *urens*) – hot and dry in the third
Pepper (*Piper nigrum*) – hot and dry in the fourth
Wormwood (*Artemisia absinthium*) – hot and dry in the second

Mars foods are chives, onions (hot and dry in the fourth), leeks (hot and dry in the fourth), peppers, radishes, rhubarb. Tobacco (hot and dry in the second) also belongs to Mars.

Herbs of Jupiter

Jupiter plants are sweet or inoffensively scented and are bluish-purple or yellow in colour. They usually grow in magnificent abundance, like the dandelion.

Agrimony (*Agrimonia eupatoria*) – hot and dry in the first
Borage (*Borago officinalis*) – hot and moist in the first
Dandelion (*Taraxacum officinale*) – cold and dry in the first
Sage (*Salvia officinalis*) – hot and dry in the second

Jupiter foods are chervil, endive, asparagus (temperate) and figs.

Herbs of Saturn

Saturn herbs have a sour, bitter or sharp taste, and most of the poisonous plants come under its dominion.

Comfrey root (*Symphytum officinale*) – cold and moist in the first
Fumitory (*Fumaria officinalis*) – cold and dry in the second
Shepherd's purse (*Capsella bursa-pastoris*) – cold and dry in the first

Saturn also rules hemlock and henbane, both cold in the fourth, and both poisons.

Saturn foods are barley (cold and dry in the first), beetroot (cold and dry in the first) and safflower.

Most of the information given below comes from Feerhov's *Astrologie als Grundlage der Heilkunst* and is representative of the confusion in linking homoeopathic remedies with astrology. The link-up is just not that simple. It would be surprising if there were not a fundamental connection between the remedies and the natal chart, and perhaps the decumbiture too. However, I have yet to see any convincing practical connections, although there is some interesting work being done. Tad Mann has carried out some innovative studies using radionics to link the two, which may well provide a key.

Sun

Asafoetida, Calcarea carbonica, Coffea, Mercurius, Nux vomica, Phosphorus, Pulsatilla

Moon

Alumina, Calcarea carbonica, Causticum, Clematis, Cyclamen, Dulcamara, Lycopodium, Mezereum, Mercurius, Natrum carbonicum, Pulsatilla, Sabadilla, Sepia, Silicea, Spongia, Sulphur

Mercury

Aconitum, Ambra grisa, Antimonium crudum, Apis, Aurum foliatum, Belladonna, Bryonia alba, Calcarea carbonica, China, Coffea, Colchicum, Cuprum, Dulcamara, Euphrasia, Gauiacum, Hepar sulph., Jodium, Lachesis, Lycopodium, Nitri acidum, Platina, Pulsatilla, Rheum palmatum, Rhus tox., Sarsaparilla, Selenium, Sepia, Thuja, Valeriana, Veratrum album, Zincum

Venus

Acidum phosphoricum, Belladonna, Calcarea carbonica, Causticum, China,

Coccus cacti, Conium, Hepar sulph., Hyocyamus, Ignatia, Ipecac, Opium, Pulsatilla, Sepia, Silicea, Sulphur, Veratrum album

Mars

Apis, Arnica, Carbo veg., China, Hepar sulph., Ipecac, Sulphur, Veratrum album

Jupiter

Arsenicum album, Asclepias, China, Drosera, Ginseng, Lachesis, Pulsatilla, Senega, Stannium, Stibium, Sulphur, Symphytum, Valeriana

Saturn

Alumina, Antimonium crudum et tartaricum, Belladonna, China, Hyocyamus, Natrium muriaticum, Natrium salicylicum, Nux vomica, Opium, Platina, Stramonium, Sulphur acidum

THE BACH FLOWER REMEDIES

Melanie Rheinhart has done some exciting and inspiring work on the Bach Flower Remedies and holds workshops, as well as individual sessions, aimed at giving direct experience of these plant essences.

An Astrological Study of the Bach Flower Remedies by Peter Damian gives an interesting and generally convincing guide to the possible links between the remedies and the zodiac. His suggestions are given below.

Aries – Impatiens
Taurus – Gentian
Gemini – Cerato
Cancer – Clematis
Leo – Vervain
Virgo – Centaury
Libra – Scleranthus
Scorpio – Chicory
Sagittarius – Agrimony

Capricorn – Mimulus
Aquarius – Water violet
Pisces – Rock rose

The Zodiac and the Salts of Salvation by Carey and Perry is a lively pot-pourri of esoterica, where mythological characters jostle with arcane titbits and astonishing word derivations, the whole liberally sprinkled with CAPITAL LETTERS and *italics* to ensure the reader's attention. Esoteric friends assure me that it is a classic and that the zodiacal correspondences with the biochemic salts are sound. These are given below.

Aries – Potassium phosphate (*Kali. phos.*)
Taurus – Sodium sulphate (*Nat. sulph.*)
Gemini – Potassium chloride (*Kali. mur.*)
Cancer – Calcium fluoride (*Calc. fluor.*)
Leo – Magnesium phosphate (*Mag. phos.*)
Virgo – Potassium sulphate (*Kali. sulph.*)
Libra – Sodium phosphate (*Nat. phos.*)
Scorpio – Calcium sulphate (*Calc. sulph.*)
Sagittarius – Silicon oxide (*Silica*)
Capricorn – Calcium phosphate (*Calc. phos.*)
Aquarius – Sodium chloride (*Nat. mur.*)
Pisces – Iron phosphate (*Ferr. phos.*)

Reinhold Ebertin, in *The Combination of Stellar Influences*, gives the following associations with the acupuncture meridians.

Aries – Kidney
Taurus – Triple warmer
Gemini – Liver
Cancer – Stomach
Leo – Heart

Virgo – Large intestine
Libra – Circulation, sexuality
Scorpio – Bladder
Sagittarius – Pancreas, spleen
Capricorn – Gall-bladder
Aquarius – Lungs
Pisces – Small intestine

COLOUR

There seem to be as many different permutations in the links between colours and planets as there are authorities on the subject. The associations given here are those used in the French colour method, 'Light and Life'. Apparently the confusion about colours lies in the fact that, at different levels, the colours change. The colours given here are at the third or mental level, which is said to be the most effective for colour healing. The colours are beamed on to the patient through coloured slides.

Sun – yellow
Moon – violet
Mercury – orange
Venus – emerald
Mars – scarlet
Jupiter – blue
Saturn – black
Uranus – grey
Neptune – none
Pluto – white
Earth – yellow, olive, carrot and black

SOUND

Tuning forks are now available from Switzerland which give the sound of each of the planets raised by as many octaves as makes them audible to the human ear. The sounds of some planetary frequencies, played on an instrument known as the monochord, are also available on cassette.

Michael Heleus, an American astrologer, has worked on a speciality called Astrosonics, which studies the expression of the planetary energies through sound and its effects. By using his methods, it is possible to find and record appropriate tone intervals for each of the aspects in an individual birth chart. He claims that the sound of the easy aspects can be used to enhance the beneficial influences in a person's life, while listening to the sounds of the hard ones can mitigate their effects, and that this clearly has an important bearing on and application to health matters.

ASTROCARTOGRAPHY

Charles Harvey has suggested that astrocartography could be used as a guide to indicate locations that would be favourable to healing, and also those places that could be distinctly unhealthy in times of stress. For example, places falling on Saturn, Uranus and Pluto lines would be either depressing or over-stimulating, while those on Jupiter and Venus lines would tend to be more conducive to harmony, protection and convalescence.

GEMSTONES AND METALS

To be effective, the stones or metals apparently need to be in contact with the skin. Don't try this, however, with quicksilver (mercury) or lead; they are poisonous. If the other gems or metals are to be worn as rings, they work best on the finger that is ruled by the planet in question. Jupiter rules the index finger, Saturn the middle finger, the Sun the ring finger and Mercury the little finger. Venus stones can be worn on the middle or little fingers, those of the Moon or Mars on the index or ring fingers.

The Edinburgh astrologer and gem therapist, Anna Estaroth, gives the following correspondences:

> Sun – Amber, Heliodor, Diamond, Rock crystal, Gold
> Moon – Moonstone, Pearl, Opal, Chalcedony, Silver
> Mercury – Agate, Citrine, Yellow topaz, Yellow sapphire, Quicksilver

Venus – Emerald, Moss agate, Coral, Rose quartz, Copper
Mars – Garnet, Ruby, Spinel ruby, Jasper, Iron
Jupiter – Topaz, Jacinth, Ivory, Orange cornelian, Tin
Saturn – Onyx, Obsidian, Jet, Lead
Uranus – Turquoise, Amazonite, Malachite
Neptune – Amethyst, Ivory, Opal
Pluto – Bloodstone, Dark red agate, Almandine
North Node – Onyx
South Node – Cat's eye

IMBALANCES OF THE ELEMENTS

Ayurvedic medical treatment is bound up with balancing the elements.
Examples of the classes of herbs mentioned in each section are given at
the end of the chapter.

David Frawley, author of *The Yoga of Herbs*, has produced an excellent
correspondence course on Hindu astrology, with a section on medical
astrology. This gives a much more detailed description of the treatment
of elemental imbalances than can be provided here.

Excess Air

As air is light, dry and cold, the qualities needed to balance it are heavy,
moist and hot.

Suitable foods are dairy products, especially yoghurt, cooked rice and
oats, vegetables cooked in oil, and some nuts and seeds. All salads
should be taken with plenty of dressing. Because the digestion is usually
weak, spices need to be used freely to provide fire.

Yeast, mushrooms, refined sugars, beans, excess quantities of the
cabbage family and raw food should be avoided. Following the Hay
diet, which separates concentrated starches from concentrated proteins
and fruit from vegetables, may be beneficial here, as the poor digestive
capacities of excess air may find these combinations hard to deal with.

The following classes of herbs are useful: digestive stimulants, sedatives, nervines, demulcents, bulk laxatives and antirheumatics.

Low Air

Here the opposite measures are required. The food and remedies should be light, dry and stimulating.

Heavy foods should be avoided. The best diet is therefore one of mainly raw food, with plenty of raw vegetable juices, sprouted seeds and grains. Beans are good, but the oil intake should be kept low. Fasting may be helpful, but in any case meals should be small and infrequent.

The most useful herbs are the digestive stimulants, circulatory stimulants, nerve stimulants, bitter tonics, purgatives, diuretics and astringents.

Excess Fire

Fire is hot, light and dry and therefore should be balanced by food and remedies which are cold, moist and heavy. As a powerful appetite is a feature of excess fire, anything which stimulates it should be avoided.

People with excess fire should eat bland foods, avoid the stimulating spices, and have little oil, meat, nuts and beans.

Raw or steamed vegetables are good, as are most fruits. However, too much sour fruit, peaches and bananas should be avoided. Milk is usually very good for these types, but yoghurt is less so as it is sour.

Appropriate herbs are the bitter tonics, alteratives, demulcents, astringents, laxatives and sedatives.

Low Fire

With low fire, the digestion and absorption of food are inadequate and therefore need to be stimulated. However, this must be done gradually to prevent irritation. Fire is light, hot, dry and aromatic and therefore will be increased by taking foods and medicines with these properties.

Hot spices and sour foods, like lemons and yoghurt, are good, as well as whole grains cooked in oil, spices and small quantities of rock salt.

Dairy products and meats should be kept to a minimum, and refined sugars avoided. Frequent, light meals are best.

Useful herbs are the digestive and circulatory stimulants.

Excess Water

Water is cold, wet and heavy so it needs to be balanced by foods and remedies which are hot, dry and light.

Heavy, oily food, dairy products, sweet foods, breads and salt, which retains water, should be avoided. Beans are good, as are most vegetables and fruits, but large quantities of melon shuld be avoided.

Suitable herbs are the digestive stimulants, diaphoretics, diuretics, bitter tonics and nervines.

Low Water

Juicy fruits and vegetables as well as salt in small quantities are good here, as are wheat, rice, oats, seaweeds, dairy products and natural sugars. Beans should be avoided, and the consumption of raw diuretic vegetables like carrots, celery, cabbages and asparagus kept low.

Because most herbs are diuretic, herb teas should be used with care and only taken sweetened with honey or liquorice. The best herbs are the demulcents.

Excess Earth

Because earth is heavy, light foods should be taken, like fruit, salads, sprouts, steamed vegetables, with spices added to increase the fire. Meals should be simple, freshly cooked, with no desserts and plenty of time in between to allow digestion to take place. Dairy products are to be avoided.

Useful herbs are bitter tonics, digestive and mental stimulants, and purgatives.

Low Earth

Foods need to be heavy and nutritious. Examples are potatoes, unrefined grains, and dairy products. Judicious amounts of unrefined natural sugars, butter and oils can be taken too. To improve the digestion, which is often poor, spices, garlic and onions should be used. Vegetables served with cheese and butter or oil are good as this helps to increase the heaviness.

The best remedies are sedatives, digestive tonics, seaweeds and minerals.

Classes of Herbs

Alteratives – Burdock, Yellow dock, Blue flag, Dandelion root
Antirheumatics – Angelica, Celery seeds
Astringents (mild) – Raspberry leaves, Agrimony
Bitter tonics – Gentian, Barberry, Goldenseal, Dandelion root
Bulk laxatives – Psyllium seeds, Bran, Linseed
Circulatory stimulants – Cinnamon, Prickly ash
Demulcents – Liquorice, Marshmallow, Comfrey root, Slippery elm
Diaphoretics – Yarrow, Elderflowers
Digestive stimulants – Spices such as ginger, cayenne pepper and cumin, and hot foods like garlic and onions
Diuretics – Cleavers, Dandelion herb
Nervines – Thyme, Mugwort and Mint
Nerve stimulants – Peppermint, Tea, Coffee
Purgatives – Senna pods, Aloes
Sedatives – Valerian is one of the best

REFERENCES

Carey, Dr George Washington, and Perry, Inez Eudora, *The Zodiac and the Salts of Salvation*, The Carey-Perry School of the Chemistry of Life, Los Angeles, 1932

Culpeper, Nicholas, *The English Physician Enlarged*, Richard Evans, London, 1815

Damian, Peter, *An Astrological Study of the Bach Flower Remedies*, Neville Spearman, Saffron Walden, Essex, 1986

Ebertin, Reinhold, *The Combination of Stellar Influences*, American Federation of Astrologers, Monroe, 1972

Feerhov, Dr Friedrich, *Astrologie als Grundlage der Heilkunst*, Baumgarten Verlag, Warpke-Billerbek, Hanover, ud

Frawley, David, *The Yoga of Herbs*, Lotus Press, Santa Fe, 1988

Lilly, William, *Christian Astrology*, 1647. Regulus Facsimile Editions, London, 1985

Mann, Tad, 'Astro*Radionics' in *Astrology and Medicine Newsletter*, No. 1, May, 1986

Warren-Davis, Dylan, 'Planetary Symbolism in Traditional Herbal Medicine' in *Astrology and Medicine Newsletter*, No. 3, November, 1987

Further Reading

Lad, Dr Vasant, *Ayurveda, The Science of Self-Healing*, Lotus Press, Santa Fe, 1984

Sawtell, Vanda, *Astrology and Biochemistry*, Health Science Press, Rustington, Sussex, 1947

BIBLIOGRAPHY

Addey, John, *Discrimination of Birth Types*, Astrological Association, London, 1934

Alkindus, *Iatromathematico*, Rostock, 1629

Anath, G. A., *Practical Lessons in Medical Astrology*, pu, India, 1925

Baker, Dr Douglas, *Esoteric Healing*, Part 111, *Flower Remedies and Medical Astrology*, Samuel Weiser, New York, 1978

Bhasin, J. N., *Medical Astrology*, Ranjan Publications, New Dehli, 1986

Blagrave, Joseph, *Astrological Practice of Physick*, London, 1671. Reprinted Universe Bookstore, Ontario, 1980

Bonatus and Cardan, *Anima Astrologia*, Regulus, London

Carey, G. W., and Perry, I. E., *The Zodiac and the Salts of Salvation*, The Carey-Perry School of the Chemistry of Life, Los Angeles, 1932

Carter, Charles, *The Astrology of Accidents*, Theosophical Publishing House, London, 1931

Carter, Charles, *An Encyclopaedia of Psychological Astrology*, Theosophical Publishing House, London, 1937

Carter, Charles, *The Zodiac and the Soul*, Theosophical Publishing House, London, 1960

Clogstoun-Willmott, Jonathan, *Western Astrology and Chinese Medicine*, Aquarian Press, Wellingborough, 1985

Cornell, Dr H. L., *Astrology and the Diagnosis of Disease*, Cornell Publishing Co., Los Angeles, 1918

Cornell, Dr H. L., *Encyclopaedia of Medical Astrology*, Cornell Publishing Co., Los Angeles, 1933

Cornell, Dr H. L., *Magazine Articles on Medical and Biblical Astrology*, Cornell Publishing Co., Los Angeles, 1924

Culpeper, Nicholas, *The Astrological Judgement of Diseases*, London, 1651

Culpeper, Nicholas, *Culpeper's British Herbal,* reprinted Milner & Co., Manchester, ud

Culpeper, Nicholas, *Culpeper's Complete Herbal and English Physician Enlarged,* Richard Evans, London, 1815

Culpeper, Nicholas, *Treatise of Aurum Potabile,* London, 1656. Reprinted Antares Press, Canada

Daath, Heinrich, *Medical Astrology,* L. N. Fowler & Co., London, 1914

Damian, Peter, *An Astrological Study of the Bach Flower Remedies,* Neville Spearman, Saffron Walden, 1986

Darling, Dr Harry F., *Essentials of Medical Astrology,* American Federation of Astrologers, Tempe, 1981

Davidson, Dr William, *Introduction to Medical Astrology,* Astrological Bureau, Monroe, 1959

Davidson, Dr William, *Medical Lectures,* 4 vols, Astrological Bureau, Monroe, 1959

Dobereiner, W., *Patterns of Experience in Astrological and Homoeopathic Treatment of Illness,* The Munich Rhythm Theory Press, Munich, 1986

Duz, Dr., *Astro-medizin und Therapeutik,* Hamburg, 1950

Ebertin, Baldur, *Kosmobiologische Diagnostik,* 3 vols, Ebertin Verlag, Freiburg im Breisgau, ud

Ebertin E. and R., *Anatomische Entsprechungen der Tierkreisgrade,* Ebertin Verlag, Aalen, 1971

Ebertin, Reinhold, *Astrological Healing,* Samuel Weiser, New York, 1989

Ebertin, Reinhold, *The Combination of Stellar Influences,* American Federation of Astrologers, Monroe, 1972

Feerhov, Dr F., *Astrologie als Grundlage der Heilkunst,* Baumgarten Verlag, Warpke-Billerbek, ud

Folkert, Dr Wilhelm, *Sphaeron,* pu, Frankfurt am Main, 1958

Gammon, Margaret, *Astrology and the Edgar Cayce Readings,* A. R. E. Press, USA, 1974

Garrison, Omar V., *Medical Astrology,* Tallis Press, London, 1972; Warner Paperback Library, New York, 1973

Gauquelin, Michel, *How Cosmic and Atmospheric Energies Influence Your Health,* Aurora Press, New York, 1984

Geddes, Sheila, *Astrology and Health,* Aquarian Press, Wellingborough, 1984

Astrologie et Medicine, HAMSA, Issues No. 1 and 2, Paris, ud

Harmon, J. M., *The Complete Astro-Medical Index,* Astro-Analytics Publications, Venice, California, 1975

Harvey, Ronald, *Mind and Body in Astrology,* L. N. Fowler & Co., Romford, 1983

Heindl, Max, *Astrodiagnosis, a Guide to Healing*, Rosicrucian Fellowship, Ocean-side, 1929

Heindl, Max, *The Message of the Stars*, Rosicrucian Fellowship, Oceanside, 1980

Hitschler, K., *La Médecine Atomique*, pu, France, 1950

Jansky, R. C., *Astrology, Nutrition and Health*, Para-Research, Rockport, Mass-achusetts, 1977

Jansky, R. C., *Essays in Medical Astrology*, Astro-Analytics, Venice, California, 1980

Jansky, R. C., *Introduction to Holistic Medical Astrology*, American Federation of Astrologers, Tempe, 1983

Jansky, R. C., *Modern Medical Astrology*, Astro-Analytics, Venice, California, 1973

Junius, Manfred F., *Practical Handbook of Plant Alchemy*, Thorsons, Welling-borough

Lancetta, *Troila Raccolta Medica et Astrologica*, Guerigli Press, Venice, 1645

Lane, Alice, *Guide to Cell Salts and Astro-Biochemistry*, Zebra Books, New York, 1975

Mann, A. T., *Astrology and the Art of Healing*, Unwin, London, 1989

Matzke, G. E., *Astromedizinische Diagnose*, Cosmopsychologische Verlag, Lauchwingen, 1985

Millard, Dr Margaret, *Casenotes of a Medical Astrologer*, Samuel Weiser, New York, 1980

Naiman, Ingrid, *The Astrology of Healing*, 3 vols, Seventh Ray Press, Santa Fe, 1986

Nauman, Eileen, *The American Book of Nutrition and Medical Astrology*, Astro Computing Services, San Diego, 1982

NCGR Journal, Vol. 4, No. 2, Winter 1985–1986

Ostrander, S., and Schroeder, L., *Astrological Birth Control*, Prentice Hall, New Jersey, 1972

Parker, A. E., *Astrology and Alcoholism*, Samuel Weiser, New York, 1983

Perry, Inez Eudora, *12 Lessons in the Astro-biochemic System of Body Building*, Health Research, USA, 1973

Petulengro, Leo, *Herbs and Astrology*, Keats Inc., New Canaan, 1986

Pleierus, Cornelius, *Medicus Criticus Astrologicus*, Nuremberg, 1627

Pottenger, Maritha, *Healing with the Horoscope*, ACS Publications, San Diego, 1982

Rao, Dr J., *Principles and Practice of Medical Astrology*, Sagar, New Delhi, ud

Raphael, *Raphael's Medical Astrology*, W. Foulsham & Co. Ltd., London, 1937

Sawtell, V., *Astrology and Biochemistry*, Health Science Press, Rustington, Sussex, 1947

Schwab, F., *Sternenmaechte und Menschen*, Bernhard Sporn Verlag, Zeulenroda im Thueringen, 1933

Schylander, Cornelius, *Medicina Astrologica*, Antwerp, 1577

Sewell, Rupert J., *Stress and the Sun Signs*, Aquarian Press, Wellingborough, 1981

Sims-Pounds, Dr F., *Seventy-Five Windows, Medical Astrology and Low Blood Sugar*, American Federation of Astrologers, Tempe, 1978

Starck, Marcia, *Astrology, Key to Holistic Health*, Seek-It Publications, Birmingham, Michigan, 1982

Starck, Marcia, *Earth Mother Astrology*, Llewellyn Publications, Minnesota, 1989

Thakkur, Dr C., *Medical Astrology*, Ancient Wisdom Publications, Bombay, 1976

Vogh, James, *Astrology and Your Health*, Granada, London, 1980

Vogh, James, *The Cosmic Factor*, Granada, London, 1978

USEFUL ADDRESSES

Astrology and Medicine Newsletter
41 Balcastle Gardens
Kilsyth
Glasgow
G65 9PE
Scotland
Please enclose an SAE with enquiries.

Astro-Analytics
16440 Haynes Street
Van Nuys
California 91406
USA
Eileen Nauman, author of *The American Book of Nutrition and Medical Astrology*, offers an eight-hour, basic medical astrology course on cassette.

Astrosonics
Michael C. Heleus
Rt. 4, Box 288
Los Lunas
New Mexico 87031
USA
Produces cassettes of the sounds of the planets for any given birth time.

Centre for Psychological Astrology
PO Box 890
London
NW5 2NE

The Centre for Psychological Astrology provides a unique workshop and professional training programme for the cross-fertilization of astrology and depth humanistic and transpersonal psychology. It holds seminars which explore the link between mind and body, psyche and soma.

The Company of Astrologers
6 Queen Square
London WC1
Tel: 01-837 4410
For lectures and workshops on traditional astrology, including decumbiture.

The Faculty of Astrological Studies
Astrological Study Centre
396 Caledonian Road
London
N1 1DN
Tel: 01-700 0639
Offers post-diploma counselling courses as well as certificate, intermediate and advanced courses in astrology.

Light and Life
Sita Mordin
33 Milton Avenue
Highgate
London
N6 5QF
Healing with sound and colour linked with astrology.

Qualifying Horary Diploma Course
Mongeham Cottage
Great Mongeham
Deal
Kent
CT14 0HD
Correspondence course in classical horary astrology.

Melanie Reinhart
12 Woodchurch Road
London
NW6 3PN
Tel: 01-328 6414
Experiential workshops and individual sessions on the Bach Flower
Remedies.

Seventh Ray Press
395 Alejandro Street
Santa Fe
New Mexico 87501
USA
For Ingrid Naiman's books and correspondence course in medical as-
trology.

Urania Trust
396 Caledonian Road
London
N1 1DN
An educational charity devoted to furthering an understanding of all
aspects of astrology, including medical astrology.

Vakschool voor Medische Astrologie Asclepios
Singel 54
1015 A B Amsterdam
Netherlands
Offers a four-year course in medical astrology for Dutch speakers.

Vedic Research Centre
PO Box 8357
Santa Fe
New Mexico 87504
USA
David Frawley, author of *The Yoga of Herbs*, offers a course in Hindu
astrology which includes medical astrology.

INDEX

and planetary hours, 114, 115, 117
protective, 40
qualities of, 118
remedies, 156–7
retrograde, 30
and Sagittarius, 121
and Sun, 49
as superior planet, 127
terms of, 123
and Venus, 59
as water planet, 80

karate, 151
karmic terrorism, 5
key significators, 29–30
kidneys, 38, 59, 60, 69, 70, 72, 73
Kobasa, S. C., 22
Koch quadrant system, 112
Kosmobiologische Diagnostik (Ebertin), 43
Kundalini energy, 44

Labouré, Denis, 115
lacteals, 36
lameness, 88
laxatives, 70, 167, 168, 170
laziness, 81
Lefebure, Marcus, 142
legs, 71
Leo
  and Aquarius, 71
  and Arabian parts, 109
  and degree areas, 88, 93–4, 104
  and fifth house, 68
  as fire sign, 78, 123
  fixed sign, 27, 74
  Mars in, 68
  qualities of, 118
  Saturn in, 32
  Sun in, 68, 121
LeShan, Lawrence, 4, 5
lesions, 33
lethargy, 43
Libra
  as air sign, 76, 123
  and Arabian parts, 109
  cardinal sign, 26, 73
  and degree areas, 95–6, 101–2
  qualities of, 118

and the seventh house, 69
and strictures, 113
Lilly, William, 33, 47, 88, 112, 113, 115, 125, 134, 137–8
Lilly's tables, 120, 125, 126, 136
limbic system, 15, 17, 36
lipomas, 61
liver, 18, 34, 40, 53, 57, 59, 62, 68, 69, 85
locomotion, 70
loins, 69
long-sightedness, 79
Lorenz, Maries, 113
love, as healer, 8
lumbar region, 69
lunations, 108
lungs, 68, 75, 85
lymphatic system, 36, 72, 81, 156

Machon, Gregorio Luis Lozano, 88
malignancies, 44
malnutrition, 41
Mann, A. T., 150
Mann, Tad, 162
Man's Search for Meaning (Frankl), 24
Mars
  and adrenal glands, 18
  in Aquarius, 71
  and Arabian parts, 109
  Ascendant, 62
  average motion, 127
  besieging by, 128
  and Cancer, 123
  and Capricorn, 121
  dynamic, 24
  as energy, 39
  exaltation of, 121, 123
  and faces, 124
  fall of, 123
  as fire planet, 41, 78, 121
  hard aspect, 47, 48, 49
  herbs, 160–61
  homoeopathy, 163
  hormones, 20
  and immune system, 18
  and insulin, 38
  and Jupiter, 61
  in Leo, 68
  Midheaven, 62